Forever Day

or

How to melt Swiss Cheese
into the Australian Pie

A memoir in search of a life
worth repeating

Hans Brunner

Copyright © 2026 Hans Brunner

All rights reserved.

ISBN: 978-0-9945162-7-5

To all whose journey is to seek, and who keep walking without a map.

FOREVER DAY

1

Please allow me to introduce myself

My parents named me Felix Joseph–Maria Fuchs. If you say that out aloud, you'll understand one of the reasons why there is a different name on the cover. I like the name Felix. I always thought I was the lucky one. My friends called me Flicks; my enemies preferred F'n F.

My parents weren't all that religious. They took my middle name from my Swiss godfather, Joseph-Maria Jost, who had a seafarer background; but maybe I made that bit up. As a boy I read a lot of high-sea adventures. J.M.J. actually was a wine merchant. When my parents ran the Hotel Lion by the lake, they used to trade with him a lot. In his later years, he moved to Catalonia, running a leisure boat hire on the sandy beach of Castelldefels near Barcelona in Spain.

I visited J.M.J. with my first serious girlfriend, Bigi, in the early seventies on a Eurail pass. Jesus, Mary and Joseph, as my parents used to call him behind his back, had grown a beard and looked like a retired, weather-beaten pirate. I guess he had grown right into my boyhood fantasy.

We stayed with him a week. He lived in a spacious apartment over a nightclub whose sub-woofers pumped Flamenco, Bolero and Fandango through the floor. Even writing that down sounds like the curse it was. I wish J.M.J had let us sleep in the boatshed on the beach, but it belonged to the municipality and they locked it up for the night. There were too many beach bums looking for free shelter. Even now, in the off season, there was a constant stream of migrating hippies stopping over on their way to Africa. The parking lots along the beach were permanently occupied by

FOREVER DAY

Volkswagen Buses, Bedfords and beat-up Renault vans. If you walked along the foreshore, you had to slalom your way through a throng of impromptu market stalls, selling colourful clothes, hemp bags, home-spun mats, headbands and jewelry made from leather and beads; all of it covered over by a sweet cloud of incense, candle wax, hash and weed, all of which was for sale as well.

Bigi kept buying bracelets until they reached up to her elbows on both arms.

I liked the hippies. Their way of life appealed to me at that stage in my life, even though, deep down, I never quite understood why they wanted to opt out of society by camping on a popular beach, milking tourists, instead of going bush, raising goats and killing wild boar; or chanting mantras in the desert, living on grass seeds and honey. Seemed kind of oxymoronic to me, but who was I to judge? I was twenty-four years old. I had finished my internship with a Notary Public, passed my exams and stayed on, keeping the accounts, writing real estate contracts, executing mortgages and administrating bankruptcies, which I absolutely hated. It was always the poor shopkeeper sods that handed over their last bit of cash and the car keys. All the rich bastards drove up in their Mercedes, showed me their empty wallet and left untouched. The Mercedes was in their wife's name and their wallet belonged to the family trust. My heart wasn't in it anymore. I decided to study some more, not because I wanted more of the same or had a clear goal of anything else. I simply liked being a student in limbo, grow my hair long, play the guitar and travel. I wasn't ready to be turned for good quite yet. Very much like the hippies, skirting along the fringes, one foot on the corporate ladder, the other in the sand. I never knew if I was going to climb or jump.

FOREVER DAY

We spent most days on the beach. Summer was gone, but the water was still warm enough to swim or take one of J.M.J.s dinghies for a spin along the beach. Growing up right at the shores of Lake Zurich had put water into my veins. I liked everything in, on or under the water.

My brother Luke and I used to go fishing in the lake at first light, when the water stirred with the muffled sounds of dawn, and we felt like the only humans on earth. A splash, followed by another, growing louder and faster, then the swishing sound of powerful wings as a wedge of swans cleared the surface and took to the sky, necks extended long and straight like arrows leaving the bow. When the light hit the water, big old men bream came up from the bottom of the lake to roll their silver bellies along the surface, as if they wanted to make sure that the sun was still there. Growing up I often felt like the bream. Diving down deep and coming up high. I wasn't an unhappy youth. At times I was just overthinking.

At the end of the week in Catalonia, the three of us got high on J.M.J.'s sweet wine and a baggie of hash from the foreshore bazaar. It ended in a fight about nothing in particular. Bigi later said, J.M.J. had made a pass at her and I had told him to zip it, which sounded about right to me. At any rate, things got heated, and he ended up kicking us out in the middle of the night. We didn't mind much. We'd had as much swimming and Fandango as we could take; we were running low on money and figured it was time to head home.

The next train station was in Barcelona. The only way to get there was by taxi. For some reason or other, Bigi was convinced that she smelled like vomit and needed to change her T-shirt in the back of the cab. She made me hold her key-ring torch while she rummaged through her backpack for a replacement top. She wasn't wearing a bra, which proved to be a big mistake. The driver must have ogled her breasts in the back mirror. Next thing I know, we slammed into a truck that had stopped at a red light in front of us.

The things you remember are not necessarily the things that factually happened. That's why the law always inserts doubt. Allegedly the driver was distracted by my girlfriend's glorious boobs that ultimately caused the accident. My first recollection was the three of us standing in the middle of a four-lane highway. The truck was hardly damaged, but the front of the taxi was a crumbled mess. By now about half a dozen men had gathered around us, watching Bigi putting on her T-shirt in the headlights of the banked up cars and the traffic light running through its colours. She wasn't hurt. Nobody was. The taxi driver spoke nonstop. Most of it went over my head. I wasn't even sure if he addressed the growing crowd or us. I don't think anybody took it too hard, not even the driver. Everybody lit fags, joked around and kicked the side of the taxi like a dead animal. After a while they got bored. The truck and most of the cars behind us took off and left us stranded on a small island in the middle of the road. We realised that nobody was coming. There would be no police report alleging anything.

Bigi angrily grabbed our backpacks from the back seat.

'Let's get the fuck out of here!' she said. I knew she was angry because she hardly ever swore.

'How?'

'Fuck if I know! We'll walk if we have to.'

'It's twenty kilometers and we're not exactly in good shape.'

FOREVER DAY

'Then do something. You got us into this mess!'

As it turned out, I didn't have to do a thing. One of the motorists knew the cab driver. With the help of the remaining bystanders, they managed to push the wrecked taxi off the road. The cab driver's friend gave us a lift to the train station. Miraculously, we got a ride on the fast train to Geneva on standby pretty much straight away. Not in adjoining seats, though. We were separated by several carriages. After we crossed the border into France, I met Bigi for coffee in the dining car. She pulled back when I tried to give her a hug. She was in a foul mood. She said her shoulder was sore. I knew she blamed me. I went back to my seat and managed to sleep some of the way. I couldn't find my happy place. A dark foreboding kept waking me up.

When we were young boys, after lights-out, Luke and I would lay in our adjoining beds and whisper worlds to each other. The world of fishing rods, the world of money, the world of whatever we could think of, we just had to hop from one to the other because none of the worlds ever held everything we wanted, just the one thing at a time, like a dark street full of brightly lit shop windows. And not just things; people, too had their own worlds. Gisela Miranda, the most beautiful girl in my world, had her very own planet.

'I'm going to kiss her.'

'On the mouth?' Luke asked.

'On the mouth,' I whispered. 'One day, when the time is right.'

'Yuck!'

FOREVER DAY

We never went there again. Well, Luke didn't. There were an infinite number of other places to be created. Sleep always took over but just before I drifted off, my universe was in perfect order and my worlds orbited in beautiful harmony. I was the most comforting feeling I would ever know.

Just about everybody in the small lakeside town we grew up in, thought Luke and I were twins. Luke was two years younger but at that time we were about the same height and build and we dressed the same. Mum always bought us matching outfits and most of the time we both hated them. Sunday was church day but only for us. Mum and Dad never had time; they were working seven days a week in the pub. Mum used to dress us up for Sunday school at the church.

I don't know what possessed her to buy us knickerbockers. As far as I knew, only Sherlock Holmes and the weirdo reporter from the local newspaper ever wore them. The reporter dated one of our waitresses. Turns out he was already married, twice over, to two different women at the same time. It was the one and only scoop he would be remembered by. After the story broke, he disappeared.

God, we hated those trousers! We wore them once to Sunday school and the shame was humiliating. We could just as well have walked around in diapers. The other kids called them turd catchers. We had to lose the knickerbockers.

We spent a lot of time at the local smithy, sandwiched between my parents' pub and the pub next door. We lived there before we moved down to the Hotel Lion by the lake. The blacksmith was a small bent and gnarled man with hands as big as frying pans. His name was Mr Yordi. We hung around his workshop all day long. When he was in a good mood, he let us use some of his tools or hold the horses. Mr Yordi was a popular farrier. Some mornings there would be half a dozen horses assembled in his yard.

I loved that place when the horses were being shod. The air would hiss and steam with the smell of coal fire from the smithy and the stench of burning hoof when Mr Yordi fitted a red-hot shoe. The older draught horses were used to it; they just stood there with their noses buried in a bag of oats, occasionally flicking an ear or a tail when a flying spark caught them by surprise. The very young horses were a lot more trouble. You could see the panic building in their eyes. Every cut of the hoof knife made their flanks flicker; every sweep of the hoof rasp made their skin tremble, and every touch of the new shoe made them back away. Good handlers knew how to keep their grip on the horse's leg and not let go, but when a horse had had enough and decided to rear up instead of moving sideways, they all jumped out of the way. I got two teeth knocked out of my mouth before I learnt that lesson. I couldn't think of a more epic place than the smithy next door, with old Mr Yordi in his leather apron standing in the middle of the mayhem like an immovable rock.

Thanks to the smithy, we finally got rid of the knickerbockers. The council had dug up a lot of old iron water pipes that needed new flanges and valves. They were stacked in the smithy's yard and painted with red primer that took forever to dry. This is where Luke and I sat down after Sunday school until the red primer soaked our knickerbockers into oblivion.

I loved Sunday school. It was the place of stories, and I liked nothing more than stories. You just can't help listening to a good story. Sometimes they were told by visiting missionaries. Those were my favourites.

FOREVER DAY

There was this one old missionary who built shelters for the poor in Africa. He had part of a hammer head embedded in the palm his right hand. I don't mean a great big sledge hammer, just a small part, about the size of a thumb nail. He told us that there were no doctors at that place in Africa, so he asked God for advice, and God told him he was going to be okay. Eventually the wound healed over by itself. He showed us his hand with the embedded hammer and he let us touch it. It looked blue and felt hard. Even back then I suspected that speaking to God really is the same as talking into a dead phone. All you can hear back is the echo of your own voice. But there was the hammer! Without the hammer it might just have been an ordinary kind of story.

I didn't really believe the stories about ending up dead in paradise with golden streets and all that stuff down to the last detail, but I guess it was okay because it sounded a bit like our worlds after lights-out. What troubled me, though, was that everybody would be there, even the most boring diehard old zealots, who probably thought they would have the place for themselves. Inevitably, they would end up running the show, just like they did on earth. They would make us colour in pictures of the saints or churn out golden trumpets and wings for the angels on an assembly line, and it would last forever and ever. Eternal life began to sound like a pretty bad story. I did not want to be the same forever, even if I was allowed to pick my very own forever day.

As a fourteen-year-old, I probably would've picked the day I finally plucked up enough courage to kiss Gisela Miranda in the schoolyard, right at the end-of-recess bell, drowned by the wolf whistles of the boys and the cheers of the girls. It looked a lot easier in the French movies my parents used to watch with us at the local cinema matinees.

FOREVER DAY

And before you go smirking at me, who's ever told you that you have to keep breathing when kissing a girl on the lips? Nobody ever told me. I just about fainted, and I can tell you another thing: I would've been happy to suffocate right there and then, with Gisela Miranda in my arms and her soft lips on my lips. I would've gone straight to heaven and told the old farts that this was going to be my forever day.

2

Cute little heartbreaker, sweet little love maker

Lyon, France, was the only scheduled stop on our way back to Switzerland. As the train slowly screeched to a halt, Bigi appeared with bad news.

'It's going to be a three hour wait,' she said.

'I haven't heard anything.'

'That's part of the problem. No intercom. Something went wrong with the electrical system. The train attendants told us.'

'Bummer! Can we get off?'

'I don't think so.'

'Why not?'

Bigi shrugged her shoulders. 'It's an international train. They probably don't have customs ready for us. They said somebody would come around with complimentary refreshments.'

'I've never been to Lyon,' I said. 'Let's have a quick look. Stretch our legs.'

'I don't know… They'll probably stop us.'

'Only one way to find out. Come on, Bigi! Grab your pack. I'll meet you in your carriage.'

'Okay,' agreed Bigi, 'but if they stop us, you don't do that lawyer stick of yours and kick up a fuss. I don't want to be thrown off this train, Flicks. I need to go home, have a shower and put on fresh clothes. Everything in my pack stinks.'

FOREVER DAY

Bigi never stank. I had never seen her dishevelled. She was incredibly fastidious. She constantly picked bits of hair, dust or fluff and lint from her clothes, rolled them into tiny balls and flicked them all over the place. She would do it even while we were having a conversation. In the beginning I thought she did it out of boredom but over time I realised, that it was just a nervous tic. She was head-turning pretty, with long blond hair, blue eyes and pouting lips. Even though she cared a lot about her appearance, she wasn't vain at all. She never wore makeup or flashy clothes. She usually put on jeans and Ts or long jumpers. When she added a head band, she looked like she'd stepped out of Easy Rider. And yet, I'm sure she was well aware of her sex appeal. She just used it sparingly. Like the time she picked me up from the train at Zurich Hauptbahnhof. I was doing my mandatory stint in the Swiss army with a mechanized infantry unit near the French border. Recruits weren't allowed to roll up in their cars until they finished basic training, so we all crammed into a train for weekend leave. And there on the platform, amongst all the other waiting war brides, stood Bigi in a blue miniskirt and a tight blue top that matched the colour of her eyes. I could have sworn there was a spotlight on her. How was it possible that this gorgeous young woman was waiting for me? An entire train full of recruits was asking themselves the same question. How did he get *that* girl? I wasn't handsome, and definitely not tall or dark, more of a mousy colour that never settled for blond or brown. Unlike Bigi, I probably was so average that most people would have overlooked me in a crowd. And yet, somehow, our orbits had crossed and our planets collided.

We went to the same high school, but she was one grade below me. I remember noticing her talking to another girl at the school oval. She was just so damn beautiful that everybody assumed she was taken, so nobody dared to ask her out. At least that was my theory. I imagined that she was there for the asking.

I wasn't really looking for a girlfriend right then. I had just finished school with good grades. My teachers urged my parents to make me study on, but Dad convinced me to apply for an internship with a Notary Public. There were only a handful positions available in the entire State, so getting in wasn't easy. This particular Notary Public gave us an hour to write an essay about ourselves. All I wanted was a job and a car, but I wasn't going to tell him that. He had asked the wrong applicant. I could cook up a good story from a dead fish, even back in primary school. If the teacher asked us for five hundred words on what we did during summer break, I would hand in two pages and he would give me and A+ and read them out aloud. I was always a writer. Until the weirdo polygamist from the local paper dated our waitress, I seriously contemplated going into journalism or become a full time writer. He put me off. He drove a beat-up old Peugeot and made our waitress pay for her own drinks. Writing obviously didn't pay enough for a decent car and a date.

I aced the test. I got the job and the car and eventually, in what I naively assumed was a natural progression, the girlfriend to go with it.

My first car was a very old split window VW Kombi bus with issues. I bought it for three hundred franks. My best friend Jeampi's brother was a mechanic apprentice. He fixed up the engine and the gearbox, while my brother Luke used his artistic flair to give the bus a unique paint job in psychedelic orange with large black footprints running from the back, over the top to the front. I didn't ask for it. At the time, Luke did a lot of sketches of feet with faces. His artwork turned out to be a failproof cop magnet.

FOREVER DAY

They latched on to me wherever I went. Doing a reverse park with a black and white in your mirrors is not something they teach you at driving school. It was just a game of chicken. They never actually stopped me, but I was sure they would pounce the moment I gave them an opening.

I took that Kombi with my friends in the back all over Europe. In France, people would shout 'pieds noirs!' when we passed. It was so weird that we stopped to find out what it meant. Turns out, 'Black Feet' was a term used for French settlers, fleeing back to France from Algeria after eight years of Colonial War that ended with Algeria's independence in 1962. Black feet with faces, indeed. How freaking deep Luke's artwork turned out to be!

The Kombi was our party-room on wheels. I had a lot of friends and they would bring their friends. Most weekends and public holidays it was full house. I installed a converter with 220 Volt output for a big reel-to-reel tape deck, hooked up to eight speakers. At full blast it felt like we were driving in a wind tunnel, powered by Deep Purple, Led Zeppelin and The Who.

My time at the Notary Public's happened to coincide with the heydays of the big English hard rock bands. A lot of them, including the only notable American, Jimi Hendrix, played the Hallenstadion in Zurich Oerlikon, half an hour by train from my parents' place. Jimi headed the bill of a two-day 'Monsterkonzert', kind of an earlier and tamer indoor Swiss version of Woodstock. And just as every second old rocker dude in the USA will tell you now, that he was at Woodstock back then, every second Swiss old rocker dude claims to have been at the Monsterkonzert. Well, let me tell you that the Hallenstadion, built to host bicycle races in summer and ice hockey matches in winter, back in the spring of 1968, had a seating capacity of around 10,000. I was there with my friend plus 4,998 random rocker dudes. All the others are lying through their teeth. That's how stories turn into legends. In reality, on that first night of the Monsterkonzert, you could have driven the Magic Bus through the hall and not hit anybody. Jimi played a half empty house. Too late to order your tickets now.

The promoter of the Monsterkonzert had brought the Rolling Stones to the same venue the previous year, and made them play on locally hired, appallingly underpowered sound equipment and provided equally miserable security. The Stones filled the venue to the rafters, and lots of disappointed fans that couldn't get in, started rioting outside. I was there with my sister. I filmed the whole shemozzle on my Super 8 without sound, clinging to a support beam from the temporary stage. I could easily have climbed onto the stage and jumped Mick Jagger, if I were so inclined. It was the worst possible amateur night for a world class act, and it ended badly, with smoke bombs and the police and security guys battling the frustrated crowd inside and out. It left a dozen or so injured and close to a thousand chairs smashed. I couldn't tell you the Stones set list for the night. All I remember is that Mick Jagger wore red corduroy pants and a puffy white pirate shirt. Oh, yes... and those little hard rubber truncheons the cops used on us like cattle prongs, they really hurt!

A year later, for Jimi's gig, the authorities were ready. By now they had gained a lot more experience with youth protests and riots all across the city. They insisted on a much higher stage, built like a fortress and flanked by security, plain-clothed cops in the auditorium and a small army of riot police hidden behind the stage. Jimi came on last. He wore his trademark pimp hat and looked as cool as the Marlboro Man. He did his thing. He might have held a guitar, but what he really played was the amplifier. Nobody in the late sixties could equal that. It looked and sounded wild and improvised, and a noticeable part of the crowd didn't like what they were hearing. Mr Cool had an untamable volcano burning inside. Two years later it consumed him. I hope his forever day didn't end up to be the taste of Barbiturates and his own vomit. If it was up to me, I would let him keep playing Foxy Lady with his teeth, until Ritchie Blackmore from Deep Purple came along to claim his forever day. He could teach Jimi a thing or two about playing the guitar with ten fingers.

Apart from some minor disturbances, the first night ended swimmingly. Not so for Jimi. He snuck a groupie into his room at the Hotel Stoller. The night porter called in vice and Jimi slept alone.

The second day started as a copy of the first, with a bigger crowd and a slight change in the line-up. Towards the end, a small group of trouble-makers wrecked a few chairs, lit a fire and started a skirmish. The army of cops pulled out their truncheons and went to war. So much so, that even the arch-conservative Swiss press next day unanimously criticised them for beating up their children with excessive force. We never expected anything else. We were the children of the sixties. Job, car and girlfriend began to sound pretty square moving into the seventies. Rock bands were our call to arms. They showed us how to round the corners. They gave us a voice and we used it. '68 turned out to be the coming of age year for the youth of the entire world. To this day, when I listen to Jimi's virtuous chaos, or Ritchie Blackmore's otherworldly magical riffs, I can still feel a young man's stir of rebellion.

About a year after the concert, I lucked out with a different stirring. Miriam, a friend of a friend I could never quite place, showed up with Bigi in tow for a weekend outing to one of the many lakes close by. Nobody went swimming. The water was freezing cold. We lit a great big fire, cranked up the stereo and cooked sausages on sticks. We drank a bit, smoked a bit, talked a lot, played cards and horsed around.

I got to talk to Bigi one-on-one for the first time. She did most of the talking. She was on the home stretch in High School. Her dad was one of two GPs in town. She had two younger sisters. She told me in confidence, that she and her family were leaving town after she finished school. Her dad had taken on a job as director of clinical studies for a chemical company in Schaffhausen, about one hour's drive from where they lived now. Bigi was going to start an apprenticeship as a laboratory technician with her dad's new employer.

'Pity, I said.

'What? The job? It's not too bad, and the pay is great.'

'You moving away.'

Bigi picked a ball of fluff from her woollen jumper, flicked it into the fire and looked at me with a tiny grin.

'You have a car, haven't you?'

And there was my trifecta! Job, car, girlfriend. I had gotten it so wrong. Bigi wasn't there for the asking; it was me who was more than ready for the taking.

She kept talking for a long time. School, jobs, family, friends, what she loved and what she hated. She could string words together like, you know, no commas or full stops, delivered with that kind of urgency of somebody who needed to spill her guts. Growing up in pubs, occasionally pulling drinks and tending the bar, I got to hear a lot of gut-spilling. Most of it was sad. Come to think of it, all of it was sad. I can't recall a happy gut-spiller, apart from the odd wedding party, when the groom or the best man turned their speeches into what they thought was a happy gut spill. It still was mostly sad.

I didn't know where Bigi was heading. I dreaded that her words would turn sad any moment. An abusive father, a controlling mother, a boyfriend who dumped her; I was ready for anything, but nothing came. She just wanted to tell me who she was. I thought about it later. Maybe that's what it was. Making sure I realised there was more to her than a pretty face.

I didn't need convincing. I was hers, hook line and sinker, but I wasn't going to tell her. I decided right there and then, that I would let her take the lead. I knew where I wanted to go, but I had no roadmap. I didn't want to stuff this one up.

In the late afternoon, I drove everybody home. Bigi made me pull up a block from her house. I assumed black feet on hippie buses weren't popular with her parents. I didn't ask because I didn't want to embarrass her.

'It's because of Miriam,' said Bigi, 'she lives with us. She works for my parents. They think we went shopping.'

'She works for your dad?'

'For Mum, actually. She's our housekeeper and looks after me and my sisters.'

'You're having me on!'

"I'm not really the housekeeper,' interrupted Miriam from the back, 'I'm just helping Bigi's mum around the house. She's friends with my Mum, and the two of them came up with the idea of me working as an au pair during my gap year. I'm going to uni once a week. I have to catch up on science to study medicine. It's a lot closer to the city from here. I don't mind the odd bit of cooking and chaperoning.'

It took me a while to catch on.

'So let me get this straight,' I finally said. 'If I ask Bigi on a date, you'll hop along as well?'

Miriam laughed out loud.

'Your lucky day, Flicks. You get two for the price of one. Bring a friend. Bring Jeampi.'

'Stop goofing around you two,' interrupted Bigi angrily. 'Miriam is not my chaperone. My parents didn't make her come with me. She told me where she was going and I wanted to come. We told Mum we'd go shopping for my graduation dress. End of story.'

I heard the back door slide open and shut. Miriam poked her head through the driver's side window.

'That was fun,' she said with a mischievous grin. 'I'll give you a minute. Get on with it. I have to help with dinner.'

'She's weird,' I said, watching Miriam ambling along the footpath, one leg on the road, the other on the curb.

'She's my best friend,' said Bigi. 'You know she's got the hots for Jeampi. Is he gay?'

'No.'

'Are you sure?'

FOREVER DAY

'Of course I'm sure! We've been best friends forever.'

'You might want to talk to him. Maybe he's just a bit slow. Speaking of slow, what kind of date were you going to ask me on?'

'Whatever you like.'

'I want to see a band, one of the big acts. I've never been to a live concert. My parents are into classical music. They made me learn the piano.'

'So did mine! I only lasted one lesson. I love the sound of a piano but I wanted to play an instrument I could carry with me. My parents bought me a guitar instead.'

'You're lucky. Your parents must have let you do your own stuff all the time. My parents are very strict.'

'My parents were always busy running a pub. My brother and I had to help a lot, so they probably felt guilty and let us do our own thing when we weren't working. They still had rules as to where we could go. My first big live concert was the Stones in Zurich. I was only allowed to go because my big sister let me tag along.'

'Okay then,' said Bigi. 'So you know the drill. At least until you make a formal appearance with my parents.'

'You mean like asking your dad to let me take you out?'

'Dad's a doctor. He might want to give you a quick once-over.'

'I'll pass!'

'You'll come around,' she said laughing, opening the car door and jumping out. 'Thanks for the day. See you later.'

FOREVER DAY

I watched her hurrying along to catch up with Miriam. She walked like a man, with big steps, swinging her tasselled shoulder bag from side to side. When she reached Miriam, they both turned around and gave me a little wave. I would have preferred a kiss but I was happy all the same. Anticipation has always been my thing.

3

The cook, the chef and the facilitator

I was halfway through primary school, when Dad took up the lease of the Hotel Lion. It was a very large property, next to the church and right by the lake, separated from the water by the main road from Rapperswil to Zurich. The middle part of the building dated back six hundred years, with later additions on both sides. It was run down and showed its age. The former owner had died. The hotel stood empty for quite some time, until the council bought it from the estate. They didn't really want to run a public house, but the Hotel Lion happened to be the only place in town with a large hall and a stage. In fact, it probably was the only such place along our side of the lake. The hall was well frequented by social clubs for band practice, choir rehearsals, end of year dinners, banquets, large weddings, stage plays and variety shows, so much so, that the council forked out a lot money to install a fly space above the stage for lighting, pulleys and ropes for scenery, backdrops, chandeliers or anything else that had to fly in or out of the stage.

Luke and I had the job of setting up the hall. Our pet hate was moving the Bechstein, a grand piano mounted on its own wooden stage with rollers. It was as heavy as a German battle tank and just as hard to shift. We had lots of other jobs, too, like stocking the drink fridges in the bar, the restaurant and the beer garden. When there was a big do in the hall, we ran the cloak room or worked the window for the waitresses. Sometimes our friends would lend a hand and sleep over. The Hotel Lion always had plenty of vacancies.

FOREVER DAY

That Bechstein and I had a love-hate relationship. Once my brother and I managed to move it into position, we'd put the lid on the prop, and the battle tank turned into a beautiful shiny black plane, ready for takeoff. Our chopsticks were wasted on it but I knew the man who could make it fly. Hans Gyr. He was one of the casuals Mum employed, mainly to take on some of the jobs we boys couldn't handle. He was older than us and studied music at the conservatorium. He loved the Bechstein to bits. He'd stay on after work and play and play, until the hall started filling up with hotel patrons who followed the sound of his music. He could play two different songs at once. I thought he was a freaking genius. So did Mum. She paid him extra to give me piano lessons.

I told Hans straight up that this wasn't going to happen, but as he needed the money, I had a different proposal: I would let Mum continue paying for my tutorial if he'd work out a score for my play.

'Sounds interesting. What play do you have in mind?'

'The Brothers Grimm Compilation. You know, Hansel and Gretel, Snow White and Sleeping Beauty, all mixed into one play.'

'Aren't you a bit old for fairytales?'

'It's not for me. It's for the school. They want to build a school camp up in the mountains and we all have to help fund it. Since we have a stage, we're putting on a play.'

'Have you got a script?'

'Kind of. More like a draft. Everybody knows the stories, anyway. I want to give it a twist with a big finale. I want all the stories turn into one. I want it to feel dark and sombre, until true love lifts the spell and brings everybody back to the life. While you get the score together, I work on the sets and props a bit more. The attic is full of old costumes and painted canvas sets on wooden frames. There is a whole bloody Heidiland forest of stage trees up there.'

'Okay,' said Hans. 'I'm in. I'll use some set pieces along the way, but I'll work out a cracking score for your finale. Something themed on *The Awakening of the Valkyries*. Wagner. Stirring stuff!'

'Whatever. Just make it work.'

I never touched a keyboard again. Hans soon fessed up. Mum was gracious in defeat. She kept paying Hans the piano lesson surcharge with his wages, and I got my first guitar.

After a few rehearsals and some advertising in school newsletters, it was show time. I did a little introduction. Hans opened the throttle on the Bechstein and we took off.

Paul the huntsman, armed to the teeth with every musket and prop gun we dug out of the attic, brought Snow White into the forest for the kill. Gisela played Snow White. She looked like a fallen angel. She had on a flowing white gown her mum had made for her, and she wore pale make-up and blood-red lipstick. The huntsman was visibly torn to bits about killing her, but eventually he told her to run and hide. Hans milked every second of it with dark and sombre music. There wasn't a dry eye in the house.

We got through the first two acts without any major hiccups. Everybody must have thought about their lines because some of them were a lot better than in any of the rehearsals. At the end of act two, the stories became one, when everybody met centre stage and embraced each other, holding hands while Rolf slowly faded the stage lights into blackout. When the lights came back on, only Snow White was left. We had never rehearsed it as touching as that, and I wished I had thought of it myself.

By the time we came to the third act, I felt pretty relaxed. We had all but nailed it. We had managed to keep a room full of junior graders glued to their seats.

I was really looking forward to the finale. Poisoned, and presumably dead, Gisela was beautifully decked out on a large wooden crate centre stage. Hansel and Gretel had just made up with their weak-as-water woodcutter dad and the four dwarfs and the huntsman and Sleeping Beauty walked on and joined them in a half circle around Snow White. In the wings, the witch from the gingerbread house was still wriggling in her oven, while on the other side of the stage; the evil queen stepmother was making angry faces at that golden mirror of hers.

Rolf dimmed the stage lights and put the spots on Gisela. Hans cut the music. Everybody waited. Hans started up again, caressing the keys, slowly building up the crescendo, fortissimo, out of his bench, arms flying, fingers hammering and the Bechstein smoking. And just when he soared over the peak of the highest of Wagner's mountains, there was an almighty bang and Luke came floating down on the chandelier hoist from the grid deck, holding on to the chain with one hand, the other holding a prop sword in his outstretched arm, very much like the archangel Michael descending on earth, with his pet crow flapping in hot pursuit. The chandelier landed with a clang and Luke turned towards the audience, saluting them with his outstretched sword like he was some kind of a Roman gladiator prince emperor. Metan, his pet crow, couldn't make up its mind on which of Luke's hands to land. It settled for the one without the sword.

FOREVER DAY

Hans found yet another gear in the piano, and when Luke finally bent over Gisela for that most famous kiss of all, and everybody in the audience thought it couldn't get any better, Rolf's little brother and his friend set off two confetti canons, powered by fire extinguishers, and the witch and the evil queen disappeared in a mass of foam and red and yellow confetti that just about blanketed out the entire stage. It was epic. It was way better than Ben Hur in Cinemascope.

Rolf turned on the lights, Hans played Cliff Richard's *Lucky Lips*, which was the biggest hit that year, and we all danced around the stage and hugged each other like idiots, with confetti raining down on us. Gisela gave me an extra big hug and left red lipstick and white stage makeup all over my face.

I didn't even return to the stage for the closing lines I had prepared. There was nothing more to add. We were already living our happily ever after. Hans played *Lucky Lips* once more as an encore, and everybody sang along.

The rush wore off soon, but we still couldn't help smiling when we looked at each other. Half of our elation was just relief that it was all over. The audience had filed out, some parents leaving extra money in the donation plate.

That night in bed, Luke and I relived the day.

'It was just a pretend kiss, Flicks. Honest! Gisela said she would kill me if I so much as touched her.'

'I don't care, Luke. You were awesome. Really, really awesome! I still can't believe you got Metan to follow you up to the fly loft. Gisela and Hans and Rolf, all of them, everybody was just great. I feel like such a fraud. I didn't do a thing and then some of the parents and our teacher came up to me and congratulated me like I had done something special and I wasn't even in the play.'

'But you did,' said Luke. 'You made it happen.'

I hate to admit it, but my daydreaming little brother, who painted faces on feet and spoke to a crow, had just given me the best piece of advice I would ever get: You can do anything if you find the fuse that lights the fire. The second best came from my mother: 'People will always eat and drink'. It would be years before I remembered that one.

Hotel life wasn't all play. We had to help out in the kitchen, too. The kitchen was our living room. It sounds homely, but it wasn't. A hotel kitchen during lunch hour or any other big do, wasn't a place where you gently arranged bouquets of greens on plates; or Helen Mirren popped in stark naked for a quickie in the cool room. It was a lot more like a Gordon Ramsay tantrum on a very bad day, because, no matter how good a chef you were, there was always a fryer that broke down, a soufflé that wouldn't rise or a sauce that didn't bind and, inevitably, the one annoying guest that sent his steak back as underdone. You could spit on it, zap it in the microwave and send it back, but you had to bite your tongue, because the guests were always more right, even if they had only ever cooked an egg.

It was a war, with the enemy sitting in the dining room, and if you didn't fly out a hundred hot lunches in half an hour to keep them quiet, they started shooting back.

It was our daily mayhem, not much different to shoe-day at the smithy, with noise, heat and steam and stressed-out line cooks sliding all over the slippery floor. Mum had to work for three because we just couldn't find cooks or chefs or sous, and if we did, they would leave before we remembered their names. The hotel was old and tired. The staff quarters were as basic as prison cells. The main cast iron stove in the kitchen was an antique fire-spitting monster that only knew very hot or stone cold. To make up the numbers, Mum employed half of the extended family and an army of part-timers, mostly middle-aged married women from the neighbourhood, who knew how to cook for and wait on a demanding brood.

School was out for lunch. When the kitchen was busy, we had to lend a hand, eating lunch while standing by the fryer, blanching two bags of fries for a banquet in the hall. We'd go back to school smelling like freshly wrapped fish and chips.

If we didn't like what was on the menu that day, Mum handed us a pan and made us cook our own. The cool room was always well stocked. Mum would put little warning labels on the things nobody was allowed to touch; the rest was there for the taking. Luke and I could whip up a cordon bleu before we knew our nine times table. Sometimes Mum, or one of the chefs, gave us a pointer, but they never let us in on their secrets. Chefs were like magicians. They kept their cards up their sleeves.

There was this one chef who made herb butter to die for. It was served with entrecote or any other fine cut of meat. My brother and I loved it spread on bread. The chef told us his butter was called *Cafe de Paris*. According to him, his dad had invented it twenty years ago and passed the recipe on to him. Nobody in the whole wide world knew how to make it. Mum was very skeptical. She had never made it herself but she showed us a roll of herb butter she had bought from her supplier. We conducted a quick blind test and the chef's butter came up trumps. *Entrecote Cafe de Paris* soon topped the a la carte menu. Luke and I were determined to crack the chef's secret. We watched him like hawks. Because it was such a popular dish, he had to keep making new batches, and with every batch he mixed up, we unravelled some more of his secret. We soon knew what herbs he used and how he chopped them. Eventually we worked out that he snuck in a few finely minced anchovy fillets, garlic, lemon juice, Worcestershire sauce and Dijon mustard. We started making our own butter. We got close but never quite matched it. Inevitably, this chef also moved on and took his secret with him. Or so he thought. Mum easily cracked it for us. He had used Knorr Aromat seasoning instead of salt. Every Swiss cook worth his or her salt, would have known a chef's worst kept secret.

Dad had taken on a second job as a travelling salesman, selling wine for J.M.J. I never understood why. The hotel surely must have made enough money for us to live on. I think Dad just liked to do his own thing because Mum was completely in charge of the hotel. The thing about successfully selling stuff as a travelling salesman is, that you have to actually like what you want to sell. Dad certainly liked wine a lot.

He took us on some of his trips. All he really did was sip wine in lots of different pubs. He would carry a case full of sample bottles, sit down with the publican and taste some wine. They never spat any of it out but they ate little pieces of bread "to cleanse the palate" in between sips from different bottles. Dad would call on maybe six or seven pubs along Lake Zurich in one trip. The calls would grow longer as the trip progressed. So would the sips of wine. It was excruciatingly boring; watching two men sip wine and nod their heads like they shared a secret or had discovered an untold truth that came out of these bottles.

FOREVER DAY

Thankfully, there was an endless supply of snacks available in most pubs, and Dad let us have them all. We ate fresh tripe with vinegar and salt; Limburger cheese with cardamom seeds, the cheeses so ripe it would melt onto the wooden board it was served on. I swear you could actually *see* how much it stank of bad feet! There were frog legs in batter; snails in a green sauce that looked like snot but tasted nice if you seasoned it with the chef's secret. If you preferred a real challenge, you went for the dried meat called *Bündnerfleisch*. It was so hard that you needed a razor sharp knife to slice it paper thin, or you could not chew it. None of this was meant to be a meal. Cleansing the palate was a big thing in Swiss pubs.

When Luke and I could eat no more and sit no more, we would go out to the parking lot and watch the cars. Eventually Dad would appear and take us to the next pub. His speech would be slurred and his eyes would be dull like the eyes a belly-up trout, and we knew that he was drunk. He didn't show it much; you had to know the signs. They always frightened me. He turned sort of solemn and kind of started talking to himself under his breath. Sometimes the drink would put a twinkle in his eyes but most times he was not a happy drunk. He always got us home in one piece but I stayed alert and ready to take over the steering wheel if Dad ever lost it.

After a few trips we asked Mum to make Dad not take us anymore. She simply nodded and that was the end of that.

By the end of the year, Dad gave up the job and helped Mum run the hotel, sipping wine with the patrons.

4

Folie à Deux

Nobody attempted to stop Bigi and me from leaving the train in Lyon Perrache. We simply followed some other passengers who carried luggage, until we found an exit. A train attendant checked everybody's tickets and waved them on. He didn't want to see our passports, just the tickets. He pointed at his watch and held up three fingers.

'Three hours,' he said. Three blasts of the horn. Don't be late.'

'I'm starving, said Bigi. 'Let's find a place for breakfast.'

There was an eatery in the station. We gave it a miss. It smelled of wet dust and hot steel, just like the train.

There was another restaurant outside the station in the busy square. It only opened for lunch and dinner. We kept walking in the shadows of old blocks of flats, until we hit a wide, slow-flowing river. There was a flotilla of houseboats and barges moored along the bank, some vessels tied to each other two rows deep, with makeshift planks as walkways between them. Some of the larger barges had proper gangways extending to the promenade along the river bank. As we came closer, we realised that some of them were floating eateries, displaying their menus next to the gangway. We headed for the first one. The river bank was busy, with lots of young people milling about. I assumed they were tourist or students. People with jobs to go to, didn't saunter along river promenades in the middle of the morning. One of them actually had a job. He handed out flyers to the passersby.

He headed straight for us.

'Tourists?' he asked, handing us a flyer each. 'You like,' he added.

I glanced at the flyer. *Folie à Deux* it said. *Food for body and mind* it added and some other French words I didn't quite get.

'What is it?' I asked. As soon as I opened my mouth, the young man hit me with a French broadside. I love France and her people, except for the grotty bits in the North and Napoleon, whose armies invaded Switzerland and messed up the gene pool. Seriously, when it comes to languages other than French, or if you happen to speak French with a foreign accent, the French instantly turn into nationalistic pricks. Over the rest of Europe, no, over the rest of the world, if you ask somebody for directions, from school kid to grandmother, as soon as they realise that you are not one of them, they'll use sign language and every bit of foreign sounding words they know, trying to make themselves understood. No the French. All they do is talk more French, just louder and faster.

I grabbed Bigi's hand and pulled her away.

'We haven't got time for this,' I said. 'I think it's one of those barges.'

Eventually we found a narrow gangway with a sign that read *Bistro Bateau Folie à Deux*. The gangway led to a mid-size canal boat, moored between two large open barges. The boat had a small superstructure at the stern for the wheelhouse and the living quarters, the rest of the deck was covered by a narrow pergola with wooden posts, beams and rafters, with a white picket fence as railings. There were great big philodendrons climbing up the posts into clusters of lilac and white wisteria flowers hanging from the rafters. Small cast iron tables with two chairs each and more pots and barrels with greens and flowers completed the picture of a very French looking, floating cottage garden.

'That's the one for me', said Bigi, stepping onto the gangway. I checked my watch. We had well over two hours left.

'What do you think *Folie à Deux* really means?' asked Bigi, as we got closer to the boat. 'Doesn't *folie* translate to madness? Surly it's not meant literally!'

'I think so. The madness of two. If I was mad and made you believe, or you made yourself believe you were mad as well, we would share the same madness. That kind of thing.'

'I don't like that one little bit,' said Bigi. 'The fate of two sounds a lot better. I read that a long time ago and it stuck in my head ever since. It sounds so powerful and inevitable. Is that our fate, Flicks?'

'Inevitably so,' I answered vaguely. 'Maybe it just means table for two.'

Bigi made a clucking sound. 'Chicken!'

An older woman had watched us approach. She wore a long flowery peasant skirt and a white tank top that showed off her tanned shoulders and arms. She must have overheard us talking because she greeted us in Swiss German.

'Are you Swiss?' I asked surprised.

She smiled kindly and said, 'I'm River Woman. I'm from everywhere. If we follow this water as it flows, we'll soon hit the Rhône River that takes us to the Camargue and Mediterranean Sea, all the way to Africa and beyond. If we follow it upstream, we'll end up in Lake Geneva and her tributaries in the Alps.'

FOREVER DAY

Not in this boat, I thought, but I didn't tell her. She seemed nice and she had given us her name. Alma.

Two tables were taken by young couples. They looked like they were having a good time. We sat down and Alma handed us the breakfast menu. It only had four different dishes on it, all of them contained eggs.

'Wow!' said Bigi. 'Did you see the prices? I'm not paying twenty-five bucks for an omelette!'

I kept looking at the menu. It was written in English, German and French. Cubes of eggs with ripe tomatoes (slightly acid); Hot and spicy Mexican eggs with crown of peyote sauce, Moroccan Red with pepper, Omelette with wild mushrooms….

'Flicks! Did you check out the prices?'

'I don't know, Bigi… I think this might not be what it seems.'

'What do you mean?'

'The menu... I know it.'

'You said you'd never been to Lyon.'

'Not this menu. What's on it. I think the River Woman is selling drugs.'

'I don't get it. How do you know?'

'This one here, the cubes, is LSD. Acid. The Mexican peyote thing is mescaline; Moroccan Red is hash, the mushrooms….'

'How do you know all this stuff, Flicks? You never do drugs.'

'We just shared a joint with J.M.J. the other night … doesn't that count?'

'Nah, that's just a plant we smoke. I mean the stuff we make in the lab at work.'

'You cook up speed?'

'Not Johnson & Johnson. A couple of the lab boys got the sack for making ice last year. I felt sorry for them. They weren't using or dealing; they just did it as a challenge. It's not easy to make it pure. I don't think anybody has ever cracked one hundred percent. But you haven't answered my question, Flicks. How do *you* know?'

'Okay, I'll level with you. Luke might have slipped me the odd tablet.'

'Tablet of what?'

'Mescaline and LSD. I never tried any of the other stuff.'

'Put a number on 'odd', Flicks. Since we started dating.'

'Twice, three times. Well, technically only twice. The first one was before we got serious. Jeampi and I took Luke on a weekend drive to Florence. We tripped on mescaline in the Uffizi Gallery. It was Luke's idea. He reckoned the paintings talked to him. In exchange for the mescaline, I had to buy him a print of Botticelli's Venus. It's still hanging in his room. Sometimes I can hear him talking to her.'

'That's it?'

'I swear that's it.'

'Did you ever take it with another girl?'

FOREVER DAY

'No. What difference does it make?'

'Just curious. If we go for the cubed eggs now, it would be a first for both of us. How long does it last?'

'Too long, Bigi. Let's not play around. I promised I would get you back on the train in time.'

'How long?'

'Hours.'

'What does it do?'

'It messes up your brain and makes you feel and see things differently. Everything.'

'That doesn't sound like a bad thing.'

'It's not real. None of it. You think you can feel something but you don't. It's all in your head.'

'What if we made love? Wouldn't that be real?'

'I don't think so.'

'But you don't know for sure. You haven't tried it with a girl.'

'I'm not going to try it on a bloody barge, either! Why don't we just wait? I can get a couple of cubes from Luke and we can take them at home.'

'I meant to talk to you about that when we're back.'

'About what?'

'Home. I want to move on.'

'We can talk about it now.'

'Nope. We're going on a river cruise first. Alma! We're having the cubes with coffee.'

Alma came over and put serviettes and cutlery in front of us. I just had to ask. 'Is it mixed into the sauce or does it come as a pill?'

'What pill, *mon cheri*?'

'I mean the drugs. Are they mixed in or do they come separately?'

'Drugs? *Mon Dieu!* What gave you that idea?'

'You put it on the menu!'

'You show me where it mentions drugs.'

'All right,' I conceded, 'maybe not literally, but it's implied, right?

'It is what you make of it.'

'For fifty bucks it'd better be the real thing,' interrupted Bigi, 'and make it fast. We have a train to catch.' She sounded angry, but I knew better. It was her you'd-better-keep-me-happy voice. She used it on me every now and then. I believe all beautiful people are born with it.

Alma served the dish in no time. It was delicious. The eggs were cooked perfectly, covered with a spicy, tart tomato sauce we mopped up with half a metre of French breadstick between us.

'What now?' asked Bigi, as we leaned back in our chairs, watching the blue waters gently nudging the river bank. The morning had turned into a bright sunny day. I didn't answer. I closed my eyes and listened to the sound of the river. I doubted that anything was going to happen. The River Woman was as slippery as an eel.

I know I didn't sleep but I thought I did. I watched the water and waited for the bream to come up. The River Woman had turned the boat around, ploughing through the whirling confluence, heading upstream into Lac Léman, past the Jet d'Eau in Geneva, shooting coloured water high into the sky. We came to a stop at the opposite side of the lake. I recognized the place. I had been here before, with Mum and Dad and Luke and my sister Lisa. We drank coffee and ate tiny little cakes in the casino, overlooking the dark blue lake that mirrored the snow-covered Alps. I remembered why I was here. Lisa lived here. In an institute with whitewashed walls and iron bars on the windows. A boarding school for girls. I wanted to talk to her, tell her that I was back on my first date, but she was long gone. Downstairs, Black Sabbath set up to play. There was a problem with the recording equipment. Not theirs. Some outfit was going to record them. The Montreux jazz festival had turned into the centre of the rock universe and everybody wanted a piece of it. The concert hall was packed, standing room only, some people sat on the floor. I couldn't find Bigi. Black Sabbath started up. Or was it Deep Purple, Led Zeppelin? I couldn't make out which, they all sounded the same, like a red hot train speeding through a station. I didn't want to listen anymore. I wanted to find Bigi, take her to a quiet place and stretch out.

'Fuck! Bigi! The train.'

'You made it Flicks,' said Bigi dreamily. 'Where are we going?'

'Grab your pack. We have to run.'

FOREVER DAY

I had no idea which way led to the station. The buildings looked smaller and streets wider. A train horn blared. I followed the sound until I recognized the station building. Bigi had fallen behind, spinning pirouettes and pointing at things that weren't there. Eventually she caught up with me. She hooked an arm around me. She seemed happier than I had seen her in a long time.

We walked into the station and boarded the train arm in arm and never let go. We didn't look for our old seats. We sat down on a vacant bench and nobody told us to move on. The cart with the complimentary refreshments came around. They offered us hot broth with bits of chicken and egg cubes, which we thought was hilarious, but we took it all the same.

The conductor checked our tickets. 'Departing, soon,' he said. I looked at my watch. It took me a long time to work out that we had made it back with half an hour to spare.

I don't think we moved from our seats, all the way to Geneva. We just sat there, holding on to each other. We didn't talk much. Words had lost their meaning and time had lost its measure. We were completely aware of it but it seemed too much of an effort to put it all together again. I let my mind wander, solving every puzzle and every question ever asked. I knew everything, could see everything and look down with pity on the young couple in the speeding train, huddled together like frightened puppies, waiting for the thunderstorm to pass.

We changed trains in Geneva onto a slow intercity. It dragged on and on, but with every stop, time moved back a notch, like a roulette ball clicking in and out of the canyons on a spinning down wheel. By the time we reached Zurich, we were back on real time. I had a bit of a headache but all up, I thought our trip to Lyon could have ended a lot worse.

FOREVER DAY

We had to catch different trains to our respective home towns. Bigi's train departed earlier than mine. We hugged on the platform. Bigi held me tight. It felt different, like she was telling me something. I remembered what she had said on the boat about moving on. For a heart-stopping moment I thought she was saying goodbye.

'Are you all right?' I asked.

'U-huh.'

'No regrets?'

'Some, but maybe it was worth fifty bucks, after all. It was the longest sex we've ever had.'

'I'm sorry I missed out. I was busy looking for a place to make out at the Black Sabbath concert.'

'You went back to Montreux? On our first date. How sweet! You know that we didn't make out then, either. Right?'

'I told you it was all in the head.'

I watched the train taking her away. I thought of all the things I should have told her. I still feared I might never see her again. The week had been a disaster, after a month of disasters. I vowed to never go to Lyon again, but I kept thinking about us and Alma's floating garden. Maybe that's what all of us were looking for, Snow White, Jimi, Bigi and me. Maybe true love was the madness of two.

5

Dinner at the palace

Dating Bigi was like booking dinner in a fancy restaurant, while snacking on takeaway on the way there.

Black Sabbath wasn't our first date. It was just the first time we went to a major concert together. Bigi never let me forget the promise I had made on our first meeting at the lake in spring. There just happened to be no major rock concert within reach until August. Anticipation was Bigi's thing, too.

After the lake, I didn't hear from her for a week or two. It felt a lot longer. Maybe I had made a mistake, letting her take the lead. Maybe she was waiting for my next move. I had none. I knew next to nothing about dating, so I asked my sister. Her advice was brutal; 'Don't be such a bloody wimp, Flicks! Ask her out.'

So I did and we went on our first date, which didn't count, because it was just a local band playing in the school hall. Miriam came along but kept her distance, giving us time to sneak in our first kiss. It wasn't a forever day moment with a near death experience, but we got better at it when we learned to breathe.

I got Jeampi to trot along on the following dates and he took care of Miriam, or the other way round. She was older than both of us and Jeampi soon aged a lot quicker than me. If a band was good, we'd stay close to the stage; if they were just okay or worse, we'd move to the very back, lie down on the floor and pash until our lips turned to jelly. I was not quite nineteen then, Bigi was just over sixteen, and we were both as green and innocent as freshly picked spinach.

FOREVER DAY

We didn't just go to rock concerts. I was still working full time but the Kombi kept rolling out every spare moment and eventually, Bigi finished school and started her job and was allowed to go out on her own, just in time for Black Sabbath and us going steady. I always liked those All-American phrases: first base, second base, going steady, and home run. Doesn't the rest of the world date as well? How do you apply it to soccer or cricket? Out for a duck on a sticky wicket, batting above your average, a single, two runs, three runs, over the boundary and hit for a six – at least that would have added a few more runs to dating, and I needed them all.

We didn't hit a six for two more years, until Bigi was eighteen. Make that a four, with the ball just limping over the boundary.

Call me slow, call my stupid, I was the lucky bastard going steady with a gorgeous, if slightly less leggy, Brigitte Bardot lookalike, and I would wait until the cows came home for her to let me enter her palace. It had many doors. Some of them she opened over time. She bought a beautiful new bra and let me take it off for a taste of things to come. Gisela Miranda was toast. I had my brand new forever day. I would re-live it at work, walking up to a young couple waiting to sign the contract for their first home, bent over like an old man because I had to hide a massively uncomfortable boner in my pants.

Like the bream flashing their silver bellies, the wonder lasted but a moment. Bigi now lived an hour's drive away. Her parents rented a run-down old villa while they waited for their new place to be built. They were polite but kept me at arm's length, making sure I knew my place in their pecking order. 'What is it again, you're doing? Accounting or Law of sorts? You might know Professor hah-blah-blah, Bigi's grandfather. He wrote several text books on law-blah-law...'

It was one of the reasons we didn't see each other all that often. I'm sure Bigi was well aware but she too, knew her place in her family's pecking order. I liked her a lot so I put up with it and hoped things would improve over time.

What did change over time, was our circle of friends. Natural attrition was taking them out, one by one. Eventually, Jeampi broke up with Miriam and went to study English in Bournemouth, where he fell in love with a Venezuelan classmate. He came back for a while but his heart had already left for Caracas. Other friends changed jobs, moved away, got their own wheels, found partners and new priorities or, God forbid, started listening to the Bee Gees.

Soon there were only a handful of us left. The Kombi, too, was getting tired of zigzagging Europe. It gave us one last trip to Scotland, before it called it quits.

It was on that trip, that Bigi and I finally popped the cherry and pickled the cucumber. Bigi had held the entrance to the palace ajar for a very long time. I believe partially because her tight-ass dad wouldn't write a script. I don't know if he caved in or if she finally went over his head; she told me she was on the pill, and if that wasn't the gong for dinner at the palace, nothing else was. The fact that I can't remember where exactly our once-in-a-lifetime, never to be repeated dinner happened, should give you a clue. Somewhere in transit, in the rain between Northumberland and Scotland and it wasn't going to be my next forever day.

To give us some privacy from the other two passengers, who slept on the benches in the Kombi, we had brought a pup tent along. Not specifically for having sex, but that's where it had to be. It was dark, wet, cramped and very uncomfortable. I can't speak for women, but I'm one hundred percent sure that most men would spend a good part of growing up anticipating that very moment. If you're one of them, don't do it in a pup tent, in the dark with the rain pelting down. I've had better sex reading Henry Miller's Tropic of Cancer.

We agreed that we wouldn't blame each other. We were both virgins who didn't know any better. I guess Bigi's dad, being a GP, could have given her a few pointers. What little I knew, I got from my sister's library. Sex education books in the sixties were written for girls only. Boys were assumed to know it all. That's why so many of us remained naturally born, illiterate pricks.

In hindsight, I blame the poor batting entirely on the fucking horrible, nonstop pissing-down rain in bloody Scotland. It was summer, for God's sake! I know I'm right because we felt a lot better once we made love in a cosy place with a bit of elbow space.

Not in Scotland, though. We had about two hours without rain in Edinburgh, after that it was back to driving a submarine along the M8. One of our passengers jumped ship. We drove him to the airport and he took off for Portugal. We battled on a while longer but eventually we turned the Kombi around and headed back south. We had wasted a week trying to conquer Scotland's weather. I take some comfort from the fact that the Romans tried for a couple of centuries and never made it, either.

6

Asking the question

With a lot of our friends gone, there wasn't much point in fixing the Kombi. I bought a second-hand canary-yellow MG B GT sports car instead. It only had space for two, three with a squeeze. I did put in an eight track sound system that could blow a hole in the car's roof, but apart from that, I was back being a solid square with a matching car, ready to gain Bigi's parents' approval. I even took up playing tennis with Jeampi, which back then in Switzerland, was almost as snobby and square a sport as golf.

Bigi had to do some extra study for work, away from her home town. For a few months, she shared a flat with a fellow worker, even further away from me. It wasn't worth the extra hour it added to my round trip. Her flat mate was an older woman, sweating on her doctoral thesis day and night and weekends, too. We couldn't move without her watching on or listening in, when Bigi invited me into her bedroom for dessert at the palace. As payback, we made a lot of unwarranted noises, moaning, grunting, shushing each other in between and bursting out with laughter.

After she finished her studies, Bigi moved back in with her parents. By now they had taken up residency in their brand new, architect designed, three story concrete bunker-type spread, set into a hill outside town, overlooking a vineyard. There was no driveway, the hill was too steep or it would have spoilt the vista, one or the other. There was a double garage at the foot of the hill, where I parked my car. It looked pretty much the part, with the three storey bunker and the vineyard as backdrop. I had to climb a long set of steps to the front door. Almost every time I did, Bigi was waiting for me at the door with her bag packed, ready to leave for a day out or a weekend away. 'Bye, Mum!' she'd shout into the house, shut the door and hurry down the steps.

If she wasn't waiting by the door, I had to ring the bell and the new au pair housekeeper would let me in. If I was lucky, nobody but Bigi and maybe one or both of her sisters where home. If I was less lucky, her mother would be there, being polite. If by some miracle, her dad would be home, he'd politely ignore me. They weren't hostile or unfriendly, they just tried to keep their roost together, which I guess, all parents do. What struck me though, was how different to my parents they were. Not richer, more educated or better housed, but distant, absent and aloof. It was galaxies apart from the world I came from. Not that my parents loved me more or gave me more; they simply included me more. They ran a public house. Everybody who walked in was welcome, and everybody who walked in with family, was family. I wouldn't have traded one day in Mum's kitchen mayhem for a lifetime with Bigi's parents, or even the worst day with Dad on the wine sipping tour for a lifetime of seeing Bigi's dad go off to work in an office she never sat foot in.

What I felt, Bigi must have felt, too. That's why her bags were always packed and, ultimately, that's why she had chosen me that day by the lake. She had told me; I just hadn't understood it back then.

We didn't see each other every week. It wasn't just because of the distance. We never were a cuddly-clingy-touchy-feely couple. We hardly ever held hands when we walked together. Bigi would surge ahead with her long stride and I would have a hard time keeping up.

FOREVER DAY

Sometimes I didn't see her for weeks, when she had work commitments or joined her parents on skiing holidays to St Moritz. When she came back, she would sport the most incredibly deep tan. It made her blue eyes burn like beacons, drawing you to the rocks. I kid you not; some random jock would walk up to us and hit on her, with me standing right beside her. Bigi would just smile at him, put her arm into mine and turn us away. It was so damn beautiful that I couldn't wait for the next guy to crash his ship. Of course I was proud to show her off. Who wouldn't be? And who knows, maybe she was happy for me to show her off. I never asked, and she never brought it up, either.

When I couldn't see Bigi, I would see Jeampi. He lived just around the corner from us. His mum helped out in our kitchen over lunch and his dad was a regular in the bar at night, drinking two pints of Lager and repeating the two highlights of his life, six days a week. We closed on Mondays.

Jeampi and I had gone through high school and studied together. For a short while we were in a band as well. He was our manager. He carried a two hundred dollar Sennheiser microphone in his attaché briefcase, together with a dozen blank contract forms to sign us up. The Sennheiser was his contribution to the band. My contribution was a full stack 1969 or 1970 100 Watt Marshall Amplifier. I bought it for an incredibly low six hundred francs in a store in Zurich's red light district. I used to go there a lot to buy vinyl LPs. It was one of the places that had two booths where you could listen before you bought. They also sold guitars and amplifiers. The Marshall was brand new but given the price, it might have fallen off a truck. It was just too good a bargain to miss. I didn't have my car with me. Luckily, the stack was on castors. I wheeled it all the way along Military Street, up Langstrasse following the railway tracks and finally into the main station and the platform. I bet any amount that I was the only man to ever wheel a Marshall stack, well over one foot taller than me, through half the city, into Zurich Hauptbahnhof and load it onto a train. They didn't even charge me extra for the ride home.

The band never went anywhere. We played a few gigs and entered one battle of the bands competition in the hall of our hotel, where we came second last. I played lead guitar and could put a few riffs together, but if Ritchie Blackmore and Jimmy Page are your aspiration, you might as well pack it in, no matter who you are. The Marshall stack ended up paying for half of the MG.

What I loved about Jeampi, was his delightful duplicity. He had the very look of a square accountant, glasses and all, but inside he was one of the most impulsive guys I've ever met. One time, he asked me to drive him to a trade exhibition in Basel, and when we saw a sign pointing to France, he made me drive all the way to Paris instead. We had next to no money between us, just enough to pay for a room in the back alleys behind the Champs-Élysées and one cheap meal. We lived off a packet of crackers for the next three days, and put our last ten francs towards petrol, just short of the Swiss border.

Another time we talked about going on a trip to Yugoslavia for a few days. Two days before we meant to leave, he showed up at my parents' place, nine o'clock at night, fully packed and ready to go. By midnight, we ended up on top of the Bernina Pass, waiting in the freezing car for customs to lift the boom gate. They took their time but by mid-morning we were on our way.

There was no speed limit on the Italian *Strada del Sole*. I floored the MG. It turned out to be no match against the Alfas, Ferraris and BMWs flying past.

FOREVER DAY

We drove all the way to Split nonstop. When we finally parked the car for dinner in a big square, we were set upon by a bunch of people, offering us accommodation. We picked an old man we liked the look of, and for once, we had hit the jackpot. He gave us a whole wing of his house, complete with a verandah, a grove of apricot trees and as much free Ćevapčići grill and Bib beer as we could manage. By nightfall we found a place with music where all the tourists hung out. The Yugoslav DJ's record collection was a decade out of its use-by-date but it was all there was for our age group. We kept going back every night. Jeampi fell in love with a German tourist and they would disappear amongst the apricot trees. She was Miriam all over again. She told me I was in luck when she brought a friend with her. Her friend was very nice, but I wasn't in the mood. I had Goddess waiting for me back home.

I don't have a single dancing bone in my body, but music does light my fire. After couple of days I just couldn't take another night of whatever the DJ put on the turntable. I offered to buy him a few records we all would enjoy a lot more. Yugoslavia at that time was still very much a communist run country under Tito. The DJ told me, the only record store that sold modern Western music was all the way back over the border in Italy. Next morning we squashed him in the backseat of the MG and drove close to 500 km to the next record store in Trieste. I bought five or six singles and LPs and that night Split moved into the '70s. I can't recall all the titles but the two tracks from Trieste the DJ played over and over and over again, were *American Woman* by Guess Who and *Child in Time* from the Deep Purple in Rock LP. Both of them start slow and lure you down softly, before the hard stuff sets in and punches you in the gut. Follow that up with *Flight of the Rat* and *Speed King*, and you have a fuse that lights any fire.

FOREVER DAY

Jeampi recognised it straight away. After we returned home, he made me DJ at a summer camp for about thirty very young apprentices of the company he worked for. I was sceptical. Very few of them were into hard rock, but when I hit them with the Split selection, the room turned into a sauna, night after night. It felt almost religious. It definitely was the most amazing mass conversion any of us older guys had ever witnessed.

Jeampi had his own car but we always used mine, even if it was a squeeze. Sometimes all three of us would hit the road to somewhere, other times just Bigi or Jeampi. They were equal parts of my life and I loved them both the same, just plus or minus the sex.

To catch up on some of that, Jeampi made me drive him to Munich to visit the German tourist from Split, Siegfrieda or Brunhilde, I really can't recall her name. She took us to a disco in a concrete bunker under a school house, almost an exact copy of the room we had used for band practice ourselves, with the same smell of stale concrete dust and the worst possible acoustics. We bolted after half an hour and got drunk in the hotel we stayed in. Jeampi had lost interest. Catching up in a German bunker just didn't have the same ring to it as making love amongst apricot trees on holidays.

Soon after, Jeampi left for England. He came back a couple of times for a quick visit. All he could talk about was Marines, the Venezuelan girl he had fallen in love with. Eventually she showed up with him. He had already told me that he was going to marry her. The visit was to present her to his parents. They didn't know that he planned on leaving for good.

He wanted to show Marines the sights, so Bigi and I met up with them in a restaurant in an old castle. We'd seen photos of

FOREVER DAY

her. She was just as lovely as she looked in the pictures. Her English was very good when she spoke slowly. When she got excited, she'd fire off a salvo in Spanish with the speed of a Gatling gun. In the time it takes an English speaker to order a cup of tea and a cucumber sandwich, Spanish speakers can tell you their life's story.

We had a great time cleansing the pallet, waiting for the restaurant to start serving. Jeampi made their engagement official by proposing a toast. Marines sat next to Bigi, pointing first at her own and then at Bigi's belly.

'We're going to have a baby together, no?' she said.

'I'm not pregnant,' answered Bigi.

'Maybe not now but soon?'

'Not ever,' said Bigi firmly, without moving a muscle. 'Not ever.'

I tried to catch her eyes, but she didn't look at me, no matter how desperately I wanted her to. We had never talked about marriage or kids. It just never came up. We'd been a couple on and off for a few years by now, and I assumed we would eventually end up like my parents. It had never occurred to me that she wouldn't feel the same way. Not ever.

I guess I should have asked her, instead of Marines doing it for me. I had my answer and I didn't like it one little bit.

I was truly happy for Jeampi and incredibly sad to see him go. Venezuela was hardly around the corner from anywhere. I knew that my life wasn't going to be the same without him. When I was at odds with Bigi or myself, he'd fix it. He had the knack. He could read the both of us better than we understood each other. In lots of ways, he was the very glue that held us together. With him gone, the walls soon started to crumble.

7

Car Wrecks

After Jeampi left, I chucked in my job and went back to studying full time. I had no idea where I was going. All I knew was that I didn't want to go back to my old job. I missed my old life terribly, though. I tried to move forward looking back. All it did was make me go in circles.

I sold the MG to the mechanic who had serviced it. He took it for a trip to Italy and wrecked it terminally on the way home. He gave me a picture of the wreck. I carried it in my wallet until it was so crumpled that I couldn't recognise the car anymore.

I got myself a dirt-cheap VW Beetle, just when Bigi and I broke up the first time. It wasn't what you'd call an official breakup. We just didn't see each other for a few months. I went out with another girl for a while, Carmen. Her dad was another medico, I kid you not, an eye surgeon. Carmen was a classmate at the academy. She shared a flat with her brother next to the Hallenstadion. I felt right at home. I got to know her mother. We stayed at my parents' new place for a day or two and her mother rocked up for an inspection. I never met her dad, even though I went to her family's place a few times. He was always underground, exploring the caves of Europe. We weren't really serious, just killing time. Carmen had just broken up with her boyfriend, who was one of our lecturers, so maybe cosying up to me was her way of getting back at him. It was uncomfortable and he gave us horrible marks, but eventually we won. He left.

Anyway, about the VW; it had the bonnet in front and it was stacked full of firewood for outings. It's a Swiss thing. You always recognize a Swiss by the stack of wood in front of his place.

FOREVER DAY

One day, the cops stopped us for a routine inspection and made me open the bonnet. They took out all the logs and examined them from all sides. They didn't find anything because we had nothing to hide. They were nice enough to put the logs back, but when the lock wouldn't snap shut when they put the bonnet down, they wanted to issue an infringement notice. The car was old. You had to twist the bonnet sideways to make it lock. I showed them how it was done. The older cop had a look and hit the mechanism a few times with one of the logs. Problem solved. It went some way towards restitution for hitting sixteen-year-old-me with a hard rubber truncheon at the Stones concert.

That day, Carmen and I were on our way to meet up with some other students at a mountain retreat. We only made it halfway up the mountain before we hit a roadblock. The snow ploughs hadn't been able to get through and the road was closed until the next day.

'Never mind,' said Carmen. 'My dad has a chalet not far from here.'

I thought she was joking, but sure enough, a bit further back down the mountain, and to the left, we arrived at a chalet, standing all by itself at the edge of the woods. There were no lights on. The place looked snowed in. Carmen said one of the locals would clear the snow and turn on the heating if they let him know they were coming. She knew where the spare key was hidden. It got us in. The lights were working and the heating soon warmed the place up. It was very nice. Fully furnished, with a big kitchen and a well stocked pantry. It even had a wine cellar. I wouldn't have minded living in a place like that. Still, it felt weird popping into a frozen house your friend just happened to have the key for.

FOREVER DAY

It got even weirder two months later, in early spring, when we returned from a trip to Venice. After we cleared the Italian part of the Swiss border, Carmen happened to remember that her dad also had a holiday house on one of the hills of Ticino. I thought it was hilarious.

'How many more?' I asked jokingly.

'Just one other,' she answered. 'In the south of France.'

This time, Carmen's surprise house wasn't empty. Carmen's brother had used the spare key to entertain some of his friends. They were all students and lecturers from the linguistics department of the university. I knew one of the lecturers slightly, as I'd spent a short stint there myself. They were celebrating something or other and were pretty much wasted by the time we arrived. I love a good feed and a drink, but they were just too far gone for us to catch up. They made us sit down all the same, and because I was the new toy, they wanted to play. Linguistically.

It goes like this: 'Where are you from?'

You tell them the state.

'What village?'

You give them the name of the village.

'Say, today, I walk home.'

'Today, I walk home.'

'Pure Zurich Highlands!' says one. 'Say it again.'

'Today, I walk home.'

'Old,' says one. 'Third generation.'

FOREVER DAY

'Older!' insist another. 'There is something ancient in there. Listen to the way he uses the umlaut. Say it again.'

I know you think I make this up, but I swear by a stack of linguistics textbooks that it is the absolute truth. I could have told the drunken airheads that my forefathers took their name from our village fountain and hung their family crest on the walls of the medieval castle where we farewelled Jeampi and buried Bigi's and my future, but I didn't. You have to be really drunk to start reasoning with a drunk.

I never got to see the third house in the South of France Carmen had the keys for. We fizzled out soon after. Bigi called in on the way back from yet another family skiing holiday in St. Moritz. Actually, it was her sister Regula, who was by now driving her own car. They probably just wanted to check on my broken heart. When they couldn't find it, they teased me for letting my hair grow down to my back and wearing John Lennon glasses, which I didn't really need. They were prescription tinted, though, to reduce headaches I frequently got by listening to linguists. Bigi didn't say much. She just stood there, glowing in her brand new tan. When they left, I gave her a hug and we were back on.

The VW lasted not much longer than Carmen. The number 6 blue Zurich tram rammed me at a forty-five-degree angle from the back. The tram driver was at fault, so I got my money back. With it I bought a very old Renault R4 that had half the floor missing. You didn't need an ashtray; you could drop the ashes right onto the road. The car also had a nasty habit of bursting into flames. The fuel line would pop out and dribble fuel onto the hot exhaust. I got used to it. I kept an old blanket handy to extinguish the flames. I would pop the fuel line back and drive on. I wasn't into fixing cars.

FOREVER DAY

The R4 didn't last long either. A woman in a red Volvo rear-ended me on my way to class. Those Swedish cars were built like tractors with hard rubber bumpers. It pushed the R4's hatch right into the back seat. The woman was beside herself. She cried and cried and I felt really sorry for her, but I didn't understand what the fuss was all about. Her car wasn't damaged at all. When she finally pulled herself together, she begged me not to involve the police or the insurance company. She didn't want her husband to find out. She gave me two hundred francs she carried in cash and promised to send me another four hundred as soon as possible. She kept her word. I appreciated the cash, but what I really would have loved to know was the real story behind her dismay.

I switched the R4 for a decent R6 I thought would carry me all the way to the end of my studies, whenever that was. Luke borrowed it for a night out. Bigi and I were watching TV at my parents' new place, when the cops pulled up with Luke's girlfriend Uschi in the back. We were sure they had busted the two of them for drugs.

'Your brother has been in an accident,' they said. 'Don't worry, he's okay and there was no third party involved. We just needed to check with you that he had your permission to drive.'

'Sure. Where is he?'

'Still at the scene, waiting for the tow truck. You have a good evening, now.'

'See you Flicks!' shouted Uschi from the back seat, grinning like the cat that got away with the mouse.

Luke and Uschi showed up a couple of hours later.

'What's the damage?' I asked.

'I rolled it', answered Luke. 'Nothing to worry about. A bit of damage to the front and a bit on top.'

'Were you loaded?'

'Naw,' answered Luke grinning. 'Home scot-free.'

They sat with us watching some more TV until they started licking each other. They'd kiss and then lick each other's faces like bloody dogs. I found it disgusting, so I went to bed. I borrowed Dad's car the next morning to check on the R6 in the holding yard. It was totalled.

Lucky for me, there was Dad. He loaned me one of his two cars whenever I needed one. Dad had plenty of flaws, but meanness was not one of them. After Jesus, he was the most generous man that ever walked the earth. He would give every hitchhiker a lift, no matter what he looked like or how much Mum protested. He'd let some foul-smelling, wet-as-a-dog bum squeeze in the backseat with us kids and take him wherever he needed to go, and then hand him a fiver on his way out. Once he picked up a bellboy from a hotel chattel sale. The hotel had shut for good, and the bellboy was at a loss what to do next. Dad offered him a lift and a job in our hotel. His name was Riccardo Banchetti. Mum was furious.

'Who would leave a bellboy behind?' she said. 'And why do we need a bellboy?' We didn't, but Dad had a wicked sense of humour. Riccardo Banchetti came with a complete bellboy livery that looked like the uniform from a marching band. Dad put him downstairs at the main entry and had him open the door for the regulars, hurrying in for the lunch rush. Mum wouldn't have any of it. She made him change for kitchen duties.

FOREVER DAY

Mr Riccardo, as we kids had to call him, bought an ancient Cadillac with fins as long as a power boat. It had no plates and came without roadworthy certificate. He parked it behind the hotel and sat in it on his nights off, listening to the radio. When he saw me, he'd wave me in. I loved listening to him talking about the places he'd worked at and the people he'd met. He could talk about famous people, film stars and celebrities he knew, and he spoke about them like they were his best friends, even if he had only ever carried their luggage or shone their shoes. He wasn't trying to impress me. He genuinely believed that serving somebody made you part of somebody. He really was the loveliest, kindest man that ever worked for my parents.

Sometimes he'd start the engine and have it bumping along, until it ran out of fuel. Dad gave him a jerry can full of petrol, but Mum put her foot down and made him promise not to run the engine too long. The badly tuned motor wafted bad fumes into her kitchen and affected the bouquet of her soups. Dad might have been as generous as Jesus' twin brother, but Mum was a better cook than the pair of them.

One morning, Mr Riccardo and the Cadillac were gone. In my mind I saw them drive over the Gotthard Pass, with four-metre-high snow walls on both sides, and the Cadillac, built for the plains of America and the beaches of California, idling along with one or two cylinders taking a nap every now and then. I hope that Riccardo Banchetti ended up carrying the luggage for Gina Lollobrigida or Sophia Loren someplace nice.

As you might glean from the type of cars I had lost in the space of two years, I was not making money and I didn't do too well with anything else, either. Thanks to Dad, at least I had a car when I really needed one. Nobody rear-ended me ever again, if you don't count the taxi in Spain.

When I ran out of money, I'd find a job. I took anything other than my old job. My sister worked for a big outfit that sold all sorts of heavy machinery. She got me a job in the repair shop, fixing large pneumatic hammers and drills. There really is nothing to a pneumatic tool. It's just a steel tube with a few valves and levers, to regulate the compressed air that drives it. The hardest part was to open them. They would arrive looking like petrified relics out of an archaeological dig. Once you get them open, you fixed six of them and you were an expert. I worked part time there for about a year, when I still had a car.

Bigi's dad, whom I hadn't met more than three or four times ever since we started dating, thought I could do a lot better. He offered me a part-time office job with the company he worked for. I never found out if Bigi made him do it, or if it was his idea. Most likely his, because the job more or less spelt the end for the two of us.

I was staying with Bigi's parents, sleeping in the basement rumpus room of the bunker house, next to the boiler of the central heating. It was a nice big room with a desk I used for my studies. Bigi had her room upstairs. She'd sneak down in the early morning every now and then. Every weekend we bolted and headed home to my parents' place or one of the rentals in the hills. It always felt like we were heading back to how our life was meant to be but wasn't.

Work was a joke. I had nothing to do. I shared an office with a woman who did the job Bigi's dad had given me. She had just bought a new place. I was so bored; I offered to move house for her during business hours. Her job was to compile clinical studies for the drugs administrations around the world. GPs who participated in those studies, got paid for every patient they signed up. On payday, the car park was full of late model Volvos, Jags, BMWs and Mercs with foreign number plates, belonging to the doctors who called in to collect. It truly was the high-end-side of dealing drugs in car parks. There was a lot of cash changing hands. I guess it wasn't illegal if they actually declared it as income. Call it a hunch; I don't think they drove all that way to collect for the taxman.

To keep a grip on reality, I hung out with the dispatch guys downstairs. They loaded thousands of folders of safety studies and registration forms on pallets and shipped them all over the world. I ended up colouring in the destination countries of the pallets on a huge map in the office. Bigi's dad would call in once or twice to check the map.

If the job was a joke, so was I. It was all back to the kids at Sunday school calling me a turd catcher. My workmate told me, that everybody knew me as the *protégé-in-law*. I believe that translates to 'little shit catcher'. I had to lose the knickerbockers, so I quit the company, Bigi's parents and eventually, Bigi, too.

Not straight away, though. We lingered on for quite some time. I'm sure we loved each other, or maybe we just loved the image we had formed of each other, neither of which was easy to let go.

I thought a trip to somewhere we hadn't been before might do the trick. That's how we ended up in Lyon.

It brought us back together until the VW days and it saw out the R6 days. I'm sorry that I have to refer to a relationship with car brands, but that's what I remember most clearly from an otherwise pretty confusing and forgettable time. Our last car was a brand new R5 we bought as a housewarming present, when we moved in together, into a small flat over the cow stables of a farm outside Schaffhausen. For a short while we got domestic, bought a cat and took her with us back to my parents' or to visit friends over weekends. After a while the cat started catching mice around the farm and the farmer rewarded her with milk, so she stayed put. Bigi was still in her job. To pay for my share, I went back working my old job, against every single fibre in my body telling me not to. Something had to give. It was us. The farmer kept the cat. Bigi got the R5. I went to Australia.

8

Cruising

I didn't actually plan on going to Australia. I wanted to go to Venezuela to marry Jeampi, even though he was already married to Marines and they had a son, Werner. Jeampi wanted me to be Werner's godfather, so my presence was required. The cheapest, and by far the most idiotic, way to get from A to B was aboard one of Lloyd Triestino's migrant boats. It departed in Genoa, went through the Suez Canal, across the Indian Ocean to Australia, New Zealand, over the Pacific, through the Panama Canal and back over the Atlantic to Genoa with several stops along the way. It was called *Express Service around the World*, which was a pretty bold claim for a 12 week round-trip. The only saving grace was the use of two sister ships, the Marconi and the Galileo. They followed each other six weeks apart, which I thought would give me just enough time to hop off the Marconi in Fremantle, do Australia, and then hop onto the Galileo in Sydney and head for Curacao, cross over to Caracas and make the sign of the cross on my godson's head; do South America and hop on the Marconi once more to return home. In my defence, I only had a map of Australia and South America the size of an A4 page, torn out from my High School Atlas.

I bought a brand new mountaineering backpack and loaded it up with a pup tent, no, not the one from Scotland, I don't know where that one ended up. I added a three pound hatchet to cut firewood, clothes, first aid kit, nice pair of cowboy boots, sleeping bag, cooking stuff and bits and pieces I thought would come in handy.

FOREVER DAY

The backpack hit the scale at thirty kilograms, which was almost half my body weight. I thought I could handle it. I had schlepped around some army gear weighing that much. Rambo type hulks only carry the heavy gear in films. In the real army, it's the little guys that get lumped with the 40kg heavy machine gun mounts. Not joking. I think it has to do with the lower centre of gravity that makes them better balanced.

To build up the kitty for the trip, I worked in my parents' pub. They had moved there after giving up the lease of the hotel by the lake. At one stage, Dad owned three pubs. He sold two and built a brand new place outside town at the edge of the forest. That's what we called our new place. It wasn't a pub, just a nice four-bedroom home with a large shed and stables on 100 acres. It had a charm nobody could resist, neither Bigi, nor Carmen nor her mum, nor anybody else that ever set foot in it. It wasn't flash, just a comfortable family home with a large kitchen, but it had the most beautiful outlook over the snow-covered Glarner Alps and the meadows and wetlands, dotted with birch trees, hazelnut bushes and fields of spring rose and buttercup. In late spring, the deer would hide their calves in the long grass around the house. Dad made us walk in front of his tractor to make sure he didn't hit them when cutting the grass. He let us build a party room in the cellar, with double insulation to the ceiling to muffle the noise. When the deer hunting season started and the hunters rocked up in their BMWs with their fancy guns in the woods down from us, Luke and I would bring up the sound system from our party room and blast them with all we got. They complained to Dad but he told them to fuck off.

The new place was about two miles from the pub, which stood in the exact centre of the town. Some bureaucratic idiot in the Department of Transport and Main Roads (TMR) one day put the tip of a pencil over that very spot on the map and drew in a new road. Mum and Dad were forced to sell. I took the TMR to court. We had a preliminary hearing in front of the judge. The TMR was represented by lawyers two rows deep, all of them dressed by the same tailor. We didn't have a chance. The compensation they offered was fair. All I could manage was a few more months' stay rent free. Dad had bought the pub from his dad; it had been in the village and the family forever. I wanted to see it fall before I headed off. Later in autumn it did fall. The local fire brigade burned it down as an exercise. I don't think Dad would have allowed it, but it wasn't his anymore. They didn't burn it down all the way to the ground. Would've been a stupid exercise, watching a house burn down. They waited until the roof was well alight, hosed it down, then stood by while the fire flared up again on the upper floor. Once those flames were out, they started over with the ground floor. It was like watching an execution by firing squad go horribly wrong. When the firies were done with the killing, the wrecking crew moved in to remove the body, and the pub was gone within hours.

We didn't stay till the end. We fled home to our new place. Dad brought up a crate of the family wine, kept for one of our christenings and forgotten ever since. We all had a sniffle and a cry. Mum asked me for one of my Gauloises, even though she never smoked. I would have loved to give her a joint, but I had none. She would have sucked it down in a heartbeat. We all cried a bit more until the wine soothed the waters. I had never seen Mum drunk before, either.

The next morning I shouldered my backpack and took off. The Marconi wasn't leaving for another few days but I reckoned it was perfect timing to say goodbye to Mum and Dad. Temporarily losing a son after permanently losing 150 years worth of history, was small fry. Sure enough, there were no more tears as I made my way to town. The backpack slowed me down, but I felt lighter with every step I took. By the time I made it to the station, I was floating on air. I was free and the world was my oyster.

From a distance, the SS Guglielmo Marconi was a very nice looking cruise liner but by no means what you'd call a cruise ship. She was several decks short of that. She was 214 meters long and could carry 1150 passengers. I didn't measure or count, I read it in the ships daily bulletin called *The Sea Herald* once I was on board.

Before you board a ship, you should remember that in a perfect world, your cook is Italian, your mechanic is German, your policeman is English, your lover is French, and it is all organized by the Swiss. On the Marconi, the cook was English, the mechanic was French, there was no German policeman and no Swiss lover but it was all run by Italians.

Case in point: the voyage started with a near passenger mutiny when it was announced that the ship could not go through the Suez Canal but would have to go all the way around Africa, adding another week to the journey. The Suez Canal had been closed for many years after the Six-Day War but reopened several months before we sailed. I didn't care but some people were counting on the express service. Nobody had warned anybody and no real reason was given.

My six berth cabin was way down by the waterline, where the iceberg strikes. I came in first so I could choose a bunk. There were three doubles, male passengers only. On the second day, the guy above me brought a girl in. Funny thing, I never actually saw her. Just one leg: white, naked, shapely, toenails painted, stretched all the way to the black warning strip. The bunks were more like ambulance stretchers, narrow with no head room; you couldn't possibly make love or pash in them without spreading at least one limb over the edge. Unfortunately, there was a roll-around curtain covering each berth, so I never got to see more of her. Not that I waited around for it. If the leg was out, everybody from our cabin bolted into the bar. She stopped coming after a few days, but by now some of us preferred to stay in the bar over night and go to bed after breakfast. I don't think I ate lunch in the dining room more than three or four times during the entire trip.

Extra meals were available at the bar. The menu featured an *Australian Barbie Plate*. I ordered one when I missed lunch. I had never tasted anything *Barbie* or Australian before. It turned out to be bangers and mash with two slices of tomato and a lot of brown sauce. If Mum had served it up for lunch in her pub, there would have been a riot.

I did eat breakfast and dinner in the dining room. There were two sittings for meals. I had chosen the second and never got to see a clean, white starched tablecloth. The dining room tables seated six or eight. I shared an eight with six Australians and another Swiss. They were all quite a bit older than me. The Swiss, Marian, was Australian by marriage. Her husband was Terry. They were on their return trip from a holiday in England and Switzerland, so we had a lot to talk about.

By the law of the sea, or maybe just because they couldn't be bothered, once you chose first or second sitting, you were assigned a place at a table and that's where you sat for the rest of the journey, even if you couldn't stand the sight of your fellow diners. I counted myself lucky to have found a table with somebody I could talk to. Terry was an interesting guy, and Marian went out of her way to translate some of the Australian words I just didn't get.

Terry was a keen collector of antiques and all things unusual. He would bring some weird little gadget to the table and have us guessing what it was. Nobody ever got it right. He showed a great interest in the two coins I wore on a chain around my neck. He told me they were Byzantine which didn't mean much to me. Mum had a whole stack of them that she had bought from one of the regulars in the pub. I only wore those two because I liked the look of them.

'How much do you want for the pair' Terry asked.

'I don't know. I never thought about selling. Are they valuable?'

'Not particularly,' said Terry. 'Fair to middling.'

'If they are not worth much, I'll just hang on to them.'

Terry looked at me thoughtfully. 'What if I swap you?'

'Swap?'

'Barter. What If I swap you for something really valuable?'

'What is it?'

'I haven't got it with me. I'll bring it to breakfast.'

I didn't have time to ask more because they started serving dinner. There always was soup for starters. The soup sat on the server in a steel pot, covered with a lid. It was already there when we sat down, so it must have been there for the first sitting as well. Nobody on our table ever touched it. There was a rumour going around that the waiters topped it up with leftovers between sittings. I'm convinced it wasn't true but that's ship life. One thousand bored passengers with a lot of time on their hands were the perfect breeding ground for any kind of nonsense. I imagine one of them just made up a lame story and let it fly, waiting to hear it come back, loaded with a hundred more lies.

Anyway, the food was okay but predictable. Meat and veggies always covered with the same brown sauce that made it impossible to detect any variation. I didn't really care. Food was included in the passage. I worked out that I ended up paying something like four dollars fifty for every meal I had, or could have had, on the round-the-world trip, and the actual passage was free. So why complain about the food?

We did complain about the wine. It was included with the meal and served in carafes. Initially one per table, but you could ask for more. We all did, and eventually had the waiters trained to leave one carafe per guest on our table. Rumour had it, that the wine was made from powder, not the actual grapes. We seriously discussed the issue over dinner. One argument was the taste, the other the sheer volume and the cost of re-supplying it in every port.

Next morning at breakfast, Terry put a small silver fork in front of me.

'I'll swap you this for your Byzantine coins,' he said.

'A fork? I already have one.'

'Not this fork,' said Terry. 'It's unique. It belongs to Gough Whitlam.'

'Who is Gough Whitlam?'

FOREVER DAY

'He's the Prime Minister of Australia, no less! It's from his time in the RAAF. See? It's inscribed G. Whitlam and that number is his service number, and down there is the Australian maker's mark. One hundred percent legit.'

'How come you have the Australian Prime Minister's fork? Did he give it to you?'

'Naw. I got it from a mate of mine. He's a furniture restorer in Redfern. He did some work for Whitlam. It must have fallen behind a panel in the workshop. When he rang Whitlam's office, they told him not to bother. The Prime Minister had plenty of other forks.'

'Is it valuable?'

'You betcha!'

'So why do you want to swap it for a coin that's not worth anything?'

'Can't stand the bastard. Never voted for Labor in my entire life!'

'I don't know…it's not even real silver.'

'You spotted that?'

'I grew up in a hotel. I know a silver-plated fork when I see one.'

'Fair enough. So do we have a deal?'

'It doesn't really mean much to me, but I guess it would be an interesting souvenir and it is small enough to fit into my backpack. I can't give you both coins for it. You can choose one and I keep the other.'

FOREVER DAY

'Deal!'

After a week or so, most of us must have realised that, short of hitting the iceberg, ship life wasn't going to get more exciting. Shuffleboard wasn't my thing; clay pigeon shooting at the stern was too expensive and afternoon tea in the lounge by the piano was just sad. There was a cinema in first class, you needed permission to go there, but it really wasn't worth the effort. All the films they showed were in Italian and older than me. So were just about all of the passengers, except for the children running riot. By whatever stroke of bad luck, I must have hit the most boring, run-down cruiser that ever sailed the seven seas. Shortly after my voyage, the passengers of the Marconi started a mutiny and the crew had to turn the ship's fire-hoses on them. Even during my trip, you could tell that the ship was not being maintained. It was already destined to be sold off.

While we all shared the sameness of the days in the prisonlike confinement that is a ship, we remained separated by age, language, background and everything in between. The first class upper deck was off limits, in every sense of the word. Predominantly older Anglo-Saxon Australian country people on their way home after their European jaunt. The middle deck was mostly Australian families of Italian origin, returning after visiting the old country. They pretty much kept to themselves and beat everybody at Bingo, because the numbers were called out in Italian first. They also supplied all the children running riot and messing up the ship's swimming pool.

The lower deck was mine. Budget travellers and, ironically, the only genuine emigrants on a migrant boat to Australia. Just about all of them were from Hungary. I got to know a few of them over the next weeks. They were mostly men in my age bracket.

FOREVER DAY

All of them spoke English, some knew German as well. They all had a story to tell about running from Communist controlled Hungary, hiding, crawling under fences, avoiding border guards and finally making their way into a UN run refugee centre in Austria. After a while, their stories began to sound the same. Frankly, I'm convinced half of them just made it all up. They were young, fed up with their country and its government. They saw a way out and took it. Assisted passage, no work contract requirements, free board in an Australian migrant hostel and every possible help for resettlement... hell, I would have jumped at it myself if I hadn't paid for a round trip ticket.

If you mix up different liquids, stir them and wait, they'll eventually find each other and settle in layers according to their density. You can look up what it's called in chemistry. On the Marconi it was called boredom, and my layer settled in the bar, at a table with two Germans, a few Hungarians, a young Swiss couple and a blank notebook.

One of the Hungarians was Istvan. In preparation for the new life in Australia, he called himself Stephen, but I liked Istvan a lot better. He was a bit younger than me, probably the same age as my brother Luke, with the same mannerisms, the same easy laugh and the same couldn't-care-less attitude about most things, including money, of which he had none. I paid for most of his drinks.

We didn't actually sit at the bar. There were a few small tables dotted around it, kind of in the passageway between the lounge and the quarter deck with the swimming pool aft. It was the perfect vantage point to observe all the ship's activities, like the Crossing of the Line Celebration, when we smoothly sailed over the disappointingly invisible equator. We felt it, though. Whenever the door opened, we'd get a blast of steamy heat to remind us how far south we had come. When the doors closed, the air-conditioning took over and we'd order another hot toddy. I have no idea why it was the flavour of the ship. Maybe it just went to show how surreal ship life was, sailing along the coast of Africa, drinking hot toddies. They weren't even cheap. Grappa was half the cost. It was made from the sediments of the powdered wine that came with dinner.

I don't want you to think that we sat there drinking all day long. Firstly, we only ever got up after lunch, and secondly, the bar closed at 11pm. Not the part of the bar where we sat, just the counter. Sometimes we'd buy a bottle or two to see us through the night, but mostly we were happy to sit and talk, play games, read or write. Sometimes others would join us, bring new stories, a tape recorder or a guitar. After a while we got to know the Italian night crew. They were tough little nuts, who could bring down the biggest and most stupid Scotsman loosing the plot after too much hot toddy. They carried little hard rubber truncheons tucked in the back of their pants and they were not afraid to use them. They would drag the Scotsman down to the brig and come back mopping the floor. Next night the Scotsman would be back and so would the night crew. We got quite friendly with them. They were a lot like the rest of us, who weren't waiting for a new morning but a new life.

Sometimes they took a short break from working and sat with us, or they showed us around in the parts of the ships that were off limits to the passengers. The galley, the brig and their staff lounge. If we were hungry, they let us fill a plate with cold meat, fresh salad or fruit that never made it into the dining room of the second class.

FOREVER DAY

In the cooler night air, I often went for a bit of a walk along the promenade deck, through the ship, down the lee side to the lido deck and round and round again, like a hamster in a wheel. There wasn't much traffic at this hour. From the lido deck, a stairwell led down to the poop deck at the stern of the ship. It was a popular spot most passengers would have visited once or twice. If you leaned over the railing you could see the wash from the propellers pushing the ship forward. I wondered how many others had stood there alone, looking down into the whirling abyss that would erase them in a flash if they fell or jumped. Nobody would know, and if they eventually did, there would be no coming back. Looking backwards was just too sad. I would have loved to do the same thing on the bow of the ship, looking ahead, but that section of the Marconi was off limits.

Before we hit the Indian Ocean, we stopped over in Cape Town for one day. I went for a walk and bought a guitar. I would have loved to see more of the city but found it impossible to ignore the constant reminders that whites only could buy stamps, or board a bus or piss in the lavatory. Not that I hadn't known about Apartheid before; seeing 'Whites only' plastered on every second wall brought it much more into focus.

I showed off my new guitar in the bar and played a tune or two. Istvan was thrilled. He wanted to learn how to play right away. I showed him a few cords and he was hooked. I let him take the guitar to his cabin and he kept it until we landed in Fremantle.

One night, Istvan brought some other Hungarians with him to the bar. I think he just wanted to introduce them to us, because they were his friends and he hung out with them when he was not with us. He didn't do all-nighters every day. We made some small talk and they took off.

FOREVER DAY

'Your friend looks nice,' I said to Istvan, after they had left.

'Which one?'

'The one with the dark hair.'

'Beka? Do you like her?'

'I don't know. I guess I do. She looks nice.'

'Okay, then.'

A day or two later I did my wondering-what-would-happen-if-I-jumped-thing at the stern, when Istvan showed up with Beka. He kind of shuffled her towards me.

'Here she is,' he said. 'Talk to her.'

I was so embarrassed, I felt like jumping for real.

'What the hell was that all about, Istvan?' I said when we later met up in the bar. 'I don't like you to go pimping for me.'

'She's no good for you,' he answered matter of factly. 'She's not going to hook up with a poor bum like you.'

I couldn't help but laugh. There was some great irony there.

A much bigger irony was coming to pass as we neared Australia. The day after my birthday, the captain announced over the intercom, that Gough Whitlam had been sacked. Half the dining room was celebrating when I sat down. Terry and Marian had ordered three bottles of wine made from real grapes.

'Thank God the bastard is gone,' said Terry. I was confused.

'How do you sack a Prime Minister? Was there an election?'

FOREVER DAY

'The Governor General sacked him,' answered Terry, 'and not a minute too late.'

'One man can sack the Prime Minister?'

'He's the representative of the Queen, so in effect, she sacked him.'

'The Queen of England?'

'The Queen of England and Australia,' said Terry impatiently. 'Don't you know your history?'

I did. The Swiss got rid of their kings in 1291, but of course you always think of the smart answers too late. Besides, the politics of Australia were probably the last thing I would have given a second thought about, if it wasn't for Terry.

'By the way, I'll have Gough's fork back,' he said.

'You said you hated him.'

'Still do, but things have changed.'

'No, they haven't.'

For the rest of the trip, I kept eating bangers and mash in the bar with Gough's fork. Terry got over it, and Marian thought it was all one big hoot.

I know what you think... he made that all up. I'll take a polygraph test that will confirm that years later I was eating breakfast with the Whitlam fork I got from Terry, but by then, I had made my own enquires and checked the service number. It belonged to a George Whitlam, not Gough.

FOREVER DAY

Years later, I offered the fork to the War Museum. They declined. I put it on eBay and donated the proceeds. Just saying. Stay alert.

9

Point of Entry

We docked in Fremantle and everybody got out to stretch their legs. I held a little goodbye party with the Hungarians in Kings Park in the centre of Perth. I had arrived at my destination; they were going back on board, heading for Melbourne. I asked Istvan for a contact address but he had none. All any of Hungarians knew was that somebody would take them to a processing centre and a hostel somewhere in Melbourne. Istvan showed me a letter from the Department of Immigration and Ethnic Affairs with his name on it. I wrote down the details. I was sure I would be able to find him.

'Keep the guitar for now,' I said to Istvan. 'I'll come for it when I reach Melbourne.'

They went off to catch the shuttle back to Fremantle. Beka gave me a little goodbye peck. I don't really know why. Maybe she felt sorry for me. I shouldered my backpack and went looking for the Youth Hostel to spend my first night down under.

I didn't realise back then, that the point of entry makes or breaks Australia for you. Had I chosen another point of entry, say Sydney or Melbourne, this story would have turned out a lot different. To put it delicately, my point of entry was the back door of the outhouse. They could have sold Western Australia to the Chinese, and nobody back east would have been any wiser. Eventually they did sell it and all the greedy bastards from the east came rushing over to cash in and build their fancy spreads along the Swan River. Anyway, in '75, Fremantle was a dump and iron ore was still mostly dirt. Don't take my word for it. William Dampier had landed around here three hundred years earlier, and I don't think he had one single good word to say about the place or its inhabitants, human or animal. On the other side of the continent, James Cook saw nothing but possibilities, green pastures, land and riches for the masses. Ironic isn't it that the wretched west was going to make a few people rich beyond belief.

The Youth Hostel in Perth was basic but nice. It had a few rules you couldn't break. You had to be under twenty-six years old and you had to stay out during the day. Easy peasy, in comparison to some other Western Australian hostel rules I just have to share with you. From the *Country High School Hostels Authority Act Regulations 1962 Western Australia* and I quote:

9. Corporal punishment may as a last resort only be inflicted on boys by the Warden of a hostel or by the Principal of the High School or his Deputy, and a person who so inflicts corporal punishment on a student shall immediately after so doing enter particulars thereof and details of the offence in the hostel punishment book.

I didn't want to be entered into the hostel punishment book, so I stayed out during the day and made friends with another hostel inmate, Ian. He was on his way home to Adelaide after returning from a two year stay in South Africa. He was vague on details. From what I gathered, he'd spent all his time somewhere up in the hills smoking pot with a bunch of Americans. When I asked him how he'd coped with Apartheid, he looked genuinely surprised. I showed him my high school atlas map of Australia, and he suggested that I should buy a decent road map to plan my trip south. It was an eye opener. It changed my plan of hitchhiking through the Nullarbor. I went out and bought a car.

Kick me where it hurts, I bought an English Morris Minivan. I was on *terra incognita,* the car was cheap and a make I was familiar with. The used car salesman told me she was a beauty, and I took the bait. He wore a black pin-stripe suit and believe me, lawyers, real estate agents, bankers and funeral directors, you'll have to work hard to earn my trust if you dress like my used car salesman.

After completing the transfer paperwork and stocking up on provisions, we took off. Ian did the first bit of driving because I felt funny driving on the wrong side of the road. We cleared Perth and the suburbs and headed for the desert. We didn't get far. The Morris broke down in Merredin after just three hundred clicks on the road. We managed to get it into a tin workshop/garage. There were a lot of tractors in there and not a single car. The tractor mechanic told me it was the clutch.

'No worries, we'll fix her up good as new.'

Ian had his own pup tent. We set up next to each other in the town's camping ground and waited for the car to be fixed. In the late afternoon we went for a walk into town. Ian turned out to be a non-drinker, which I found amazing for somebody who had spent two years up a hill in South Africa smoking pot. Actually, that might have explained it. No pubs. I found one. *The Commercial*.

When I entered the public bar, there was this awkward moment when everybody stopped talking and stared at the door, and I felt like turning around to see who else was coming in. The moment passed. I ordered a beer. The one thing I have learned travelling in foreign countries is, do as the locals do. I pointed at the glass of one of the drinkers and said, 'I'll have one of those.' I blended right in.

Of course I didn't, once they caught my accent and as it turned out, the bar was full of linguists who wanted to play. You can insert the colloquial Aussie slang bits if you feel like it. It goes like this:

'Where you from?'

'Switzerland.'

'Never been there myself. How to you like Australia?'

'Just arrived a few days ago. I liked Perth a lot. Kings Park. It's a beautiful city.'

'So what brings you here?'

'My car broke down.'

'What sort of car?'

'Morris Minivan.'

'Insert, insert, insert, poofta car! Should have bought a Kingswood. Don't they make cars in Sweden?'

'Switzerland.'

'As I said, Sweden. Volvo, that's it! Volvos and beautiful blond girls. ABBA. You ever met them?'

'Can't say I have.'

'If you ever run into them, say hello from Charlie. Love their songs.'

'I will.'

'How do you like the beer? Not too cold for you?'

'Beer is perfect.'

FOREVER DAY

'Good on you, mate. Have another!'

I know what you think I thought, but you're wrong. I was half his age and he probably thought I was a bum, but he still spoke to me. He bought me a beer and I bought him another and who cares if I was Swedish or Australian or whatever. In Switzerland it would have taken me a week just to get on first name base. Be warned, though, it's a quiz. If you get an answer wrong, they buzz you out and tell you to go back to where you came from, which sounds funnier if it comes from a bloke who thinks it's Sweden. Anyway, that evening I felt more Australian than Swedish, until I came back to the tent, where Ian told me I was up shit creek.

'I went past the garage,' he said. 'Those guys have no clue what they are doing.'

'What do you mean?'

'I mean they've taken your car apart and spread the bits and pieces all over the workshop floor, trying to find the broken one. Look, Flicks, I can't hang around for days on end. I need to be back in Adelaide for my sister's wedding. If I take the Indian Pacific to Adelaide, I should make it in time. Can you lend me the fare? I'll pay you back.'

'Sure. How much do you need?'

'Fifty should do it. I'll send you a money order as soon as I'm home. Have you got a forwarding address?'

'Send it poste restante care of GPO Melbourne. I have to go there to pick up my guitar.'

FOREVER DAY

We exchanged addresses as you do on the road, but you already know that you'll never write or call. In fairness, Ian did send that money order to the GPO.

I got to share a few more drinks with Charlie. He worked for one of those public works departments where one man with a shovel does all the work while five others watch on. I wouldn't have picked Charlie as the guy with the shovel but he was good company. We watched a lot of TV on a black and white in the bar. Cricket mostly. I had no clue what it was all about. It was played in slow motion and it took days for it to finish. Two men with a bat did all the work in the middle, while eleven others stood around watching on, or handing out autographs to the fans over the fence. Two or three days later, Charlie had taught me the basics of the game, Ian Chappell shook hands with Clive Lloyd, and my car was finally ready to go. Australia had won, I lost big time.

Whatever the tractor mechanic had fixed, broke again with a loud bang, and the Morris died its second death. I was stranded somewhere on the Great Eastern Highway between Merredin and Kalgoorlie. I know now that you don't call that stretch a desert, but to me then, freshly from the lush green hills and valleys of Europe, it looked like a dry-as-a-camel's-fart bloody great big desert, full of red dirt and sand and curious small pebbles with holes. Okay, there were a few shrubs and low trees as well; just enough to push the car out of sight, but that came later.

Initially I just sat there cursing. There was not much traffic in either direction. I had the bonnet up, so just about every car or truck that came along stopped, and the drivers asked me if I needed help. I was still trying to work out what to do next, so I declined. It did make me feel a lot better towards Australians in general. So far it had been a draw, with two wins and two dead losses.

After a while I felt embarrassed to have everybody stop, even if they were long gaps in between. I asked the next guy who stopped to help me push the Morris away from the road into the bushes. He asked me what I was going to do with it. I had no idea but after he left, a plan slowly started building in my mind. I had provisions for seven days or more. I couldn't take them with me. I had a car to sleep in. I was in the middle of nowhere; I had a lot of time on my hands, and I was alone in complete and utter silence. When all the noise stops, you can only hear your own thoughts. Some people hate that. I don't. What I hate is boredom. I need something to do. For me, thinking is the same as writing. I do it all the time. I can write a whole play or argue a complex court case on my way to town. I assume most people do it. They just never talk about it, and they don't actually write it down. I did. I stayed on that spot for most of a week until I ran out of pages in my notepad.

I built a shade shelter around the car, cutting down branches with my hatchet and stretching the pup tent over them. I pulled out the backseat and put all my provisions into the front, giving me enough room to sleep in the back. I felt like Robinson Crusoe on a desert island. If there had been a lake for fishing, I would have stayed for good.

Actually, there was a huge lake full of water just behind me. Unfortunately it was all encased in a large steel pipe, stretching close to 600 kilometres from Perth to the goldfields of Kalgoorlie. I often climbed up top and walked along the pipeline heading east or west. Sometimes I stretched out on top of the steel pipe, glinting at the sun in an endless blue sky. I had never experienced the enormity of a land under a sky that stretched right into the universe. If I were the first human looking up, I would have thought the earth was flat and everything on it, the land, the sky and I, were standing still, while the sun slowly orbited around us.

On one of my pipeline walks, I came across a little oasis of lush green with a little pool of water. I couldn't find a leak but no doubt the water had come from the pipeline. It became my favourite spot. When I sat very still, snakes, lizards, birds, butterflies, and the odd goanna would join me. When I came across the first of those huge monitor lizards, I bolted left and it bolted right. I think we were both as scared as each other. It was as big a bloody dinosaur!

If the pipe was my walk of wonder and beauty, my other time on the road was the exact opposite. The first large kangaroo I saw up close was roadkill. So was my second and third... I gave up counting after and diverged back to the pipeline whenever I smelt another carcass waiting ahead. Apart from the roadkill, the highway shoulders were also the world's biggest dumping ground of empty bottles and drink cans. I wish I could have taken pictures, because nobody I told about it later would believe me. I'm talking uncountable thousands of trash bottles and cans, rolled down the verge and forming a solid carpet, stretching from horizon to horizon on both sides of the road. At dusk, the last sunlight made them glitter and sparkle, like two strings of fairy lights lining the highway. With wonder in mind and love in the heart, even grumpy old William Dampier could have found beauty in trash.

I was almost sad to leave, but after a week my notepad was full and my provision ran low. I loaded up my backpack and stood on the side of the road, ready to put up my thumb for the next car. I had to wait a while but eventually one came and it stopped. I've hitchhiked a bit so I was surprised when the driver didn't just wind down the window and ask me where I was heading. Instead he jumped out of the car and walked a few steps away to urinate on the empties on the verge. He wasn't much older than me. He had short blond hair and he wore a button up khaki shirt with two breast pockets. He looked like a solid square, not the type of guy I would make friends with, but all I wanted was a lift. I got the feeling that he hadn't really stopped for me.

After he finished his business, he turned around and pointed to the Morris in the bushes.

'Yours?' he asked.

I nodded agreement.

'What's wrong with it?'

'I think it's the clutch. The engine runs but I can't put it in gear.'

'Can be fixed,' he said confidentially. 'Having it towed?'

'How far is it to Kalgoorlie?' I asked. I didn't want to tell him about the tractor mechanic in Merredin.

'Sixty miles.'

'I don't know… I have to make arrangements in Kalgoorlie.'

'Want to sell it?'

'To you?'

'Nobody else here, is there?'

'How much do you offer?'

FOREVER DAY

He looked at me, and then he turned around and walked back to the Morris.

'It's still got five months' worth of rego on it,' he shouted. 'You got the papers?'

'I have a copy of the transfer of ownership and a copy of the roadworthy certificate, if that's what you mean.'

'That'll do. Mind if I start her up?'

'Key is in the lock.'

'You're the trusting sort?'

'I told you the car wasn't going anywhere.'

He started the engine, revved it up a few times and crunched the gears a few times more.

'Nothing wrong with the motor,' he said after walking back to me and handing me the car key. 'I'll give you two hundred for it.'

'Five.'

'Not a chance.'

'I paid one thousand plus transfer.'

'That's before the clutch.'

'You can get a new clutch for one hundred and fifty.'

He looked at me suspiciously.

'For a blow-in you're pretty clued up about prices. Where you from? Germany?'

'Sweden.'

FOREVER DAY

'I had you down for a bloody Kraut.'

'Five hundred. Cash. Take it or leave it.'

'I don't carry that sort of money with me. Would you take a shotty for it? It's worth a lot more than your bloody old car.'

'What's a shotty?'

'You don' know how to piss, do you? It's a shotgun.'

'Can you picture me hitchhiking with a shotgun on my pack?'

'You can always flog it off. Matter of fact, I got two of them in my boot. I'm on my way to Kalgoorlie to sell them. Want to have a peek?'

'Not really. Look, I have to go to Kalgoorlie and I need lift. If you want to buy my car you'll have to come up with the cash. That's my last word.'

'Fair enough. Here is what we'll do: I drive you to Kalgoorlie, I sell my guns and give you the cash there in exchange for the key and the papers. How does that work for you?'

'Fine with me.'

We took off into the afternoon. I think his car was a Datsun but I could be wrong. He told me his name was Gus and he lived in a place not far from where I had broken down. I gathered it was a farm, because he spoke of cattle and dogs and shooting pests like rabbits and roos. He drove as fast as the car would go. I was scared shitless. After a while, the car started to smell real bad and I could see white smoke drifting from the edge of the bonnet.

'You need to stop,' I said. 'You're cooking the engine.'

FOREVER DAY

'Bloody Japanese bit of crap!' he said. 'Can't stop or we won't make it before the gun shop closes.'

'I've got water in my pack. You have to stop. Now!'

He kept driving. I watched the red needle on the temperature gauge. It had been stuck above the top mark for a long time. I was waiting for a warning light to blink, and alarm to go off or the engine to spectacularly explode, but nothing happened. The car just died and quietly rolled out and, as incredible as it sounds, I was stranded for the third time in ten days, on a stretch of road a Kingswood could have done in a morning's work. Point of entry. You just can't make it up.

Gus was not a car guy. That much we had in common. He opened the bonnet and we looked at the lava inside. There wasn't much to see, but the heat and the smell of burned rubber and plastic and whatever else makes an engine run, was something else. The hot engine block made a very loud ticking sound.

'Got that water ready?' asked Gus.

By the time I got the two water bottles out of my pack, Gus had managed to open the radiator cap. There were two little hisses and two tiny little puffs of steam when he emptied the bottles into the radiator. It had swallowed the water without a trace.

By this time, a truck had pulled up and the driver came over for a look.

'You burned all the oil in the engine,' he said. 'I've got a five-gallon drum in the cab. That might do the trick.'

He used one of the trash bottles from the verge as funnel, and while he poured, the neck of the bottle melted right into the engine. It looked like glass but it might have been plastic, judging by how quickly it had melted. By now, three non-car guys standing around the barbequed engine realised that their goose was cooked.

The truck driver offered us a lift into Kalgoorlie. It was a squeeze but we made it. Gus, me, my backpack and two shotguns. We stayed in a caravan park on the outskirts of Kalgoorlie. Gus in an overnight van, me in my pup tent. Next morning we walked into town. Gus went to the gun shop; I went to the train station to book a ticket on the Indian Pacific to Adelaide. Gus came good with the cash. I went to a newsagency and bought a large notebook. That evening in my tent, I added the last day to the last chapter. Not that I would ever forget it. Writing it down just made it feel a lot more real.

FOREVER DAY

10

Living on the thumb

I never bought the hitchhikers guide to Europe or anywhere else. I had come up with my own guide that didn't require any reading. Make yourself presentable; don't hide your backpack, your guitar or your boyfriend, put out your thumb, or your hand, or just one finger, if you want to play it cool. But most of all: look interested, like you really want that lift from that very driver.

Before Ivan Milat and a few other murderous bastards wrecked it for all of us, hitchhiking used to be a great way of getting around on a budget. Granted, even if you take Milat & Co out of the equation, there always were other risks. Like having Gus as your driver; like standing on the roadside as target for a panel van full of drunken louts, throwing half full beer cans at you. Roadkill always got to me. West of the Black Stump it's a defining feature of the landscape. There are just too many long stretches of highway in Australia, and too few men with a shovel to keep them tidy.

I used to hitchhike quite a bit with Jeampi in Europe. It was just to go somewhere. Utilitarian. Save money, get there. Hitchhiking on your own adds a different component: get somewhere, have company, somebody to listen to and talk to, make friends with, learn something new. It requires you to let your ride decide where you go. You don't tell them where you're heading. You ask them, where they're going. And if the folks will have you, then they'll have you. Sorry, I nicked that one from Steely Dan. They must have hitchhiked a lot, too.

The ride to Adelaide on the Indian Pacific was pure bliss. I mean it from the bottom of my heart. I think these days it will set you back a month's wage or more, back then it was dirt cheap. After the Marconi, after the slowest six hundred clicks in my life, the train was just pure luxury. Picture a dining car with white table cloths and starched napkins, friendly staff turning down your sleeping bunk and waking you up with a cup of tea in the morning, watching the Nullarbor Plain stretching out behind a glass window in the comfort of an air conditioned carriage.

Adelaide shares its name with Swiss Heidi. Bet you didn't know that. It's actually quite a fitting. Heidi town. My dad had always dreamed of coming here. To the Barossa Valley. Before I left, he had given me the address of one of his wine maker friends, who had settled here ages ago. I didn't really feel like popping in on somebody I had never met. I did have Ian's address. He'd only had a head start of a good week on me, and I didn't want to barge in like a debt collector. I did like Heidi town a lot. Like Perth, it was just the right size for a pedestrian to get around. It's make or break if you travel on foot on a budget. It still kills you if you carry a backpack as heavy as a dead pony. I know because we had one. He was called Bijou. He contracted strangles. When he got very sick, I tried to hold him up but he fell on me and knocked out three more of my teeth. Dad had to put him down. I'm still paying for the carnage he left in my mouth.

Anyway, it was time to lighten the load, in the gardens of the Adelaide Festival Centre, so new that it still smelled of fresh paint. I put everything I carried out on the grass and took inventory. The cowboy boots went, the hatchet, most of my cooking gear, most of the clothes I didn't have on my back, my first aid kit, two books and all the stuff I'd packed without remembering why.

FOREVER DAY

Being a tidy Swiss, I stuffed it all into a rubbish bin. I could just as well have done the Australian thing and dumped them on the grass. By the time I walked off with my considerably lighter pack; two old guys were already fighting over my cowboy boots and the hatchet out of the bin.

I can't recall where the first hitch took me, or the second or third. I can remember who gave me a lift. A young couple on their way to a beach holiday. An old couple towing a great big caravan. Hitching a caravan was a first for me. They put my pack in the caravan and let me ride in the back of their car. They were the loveliest people. I think they must have felt protective towards a lone young man on the road. It was slow going. Every so often they'd pull up on the roadside, get a table and chairs out of the caravan and set up for morning tea, elevenses, lunch, afternoon tea, or just a cuppa for the hell of it. If that slowed us down, the toilet breaks resulting from the tea breaks just added up to more stops. I didn't mind one little bit. They were great company and had a story for just about everything we encountered along the way. When they stopped for the night, I set up my tent right next to their caravan.

Next day, somewhere along the way to the Victorian border, we came across a hitchhiker with a Swiss flag on his pack. I never warmed to the idea of carrying your nationality on your back. I don't think many Australians would have recognised the Swiss flag at all. They probably would have thought you were touring Australia on a mission for the Red Cross. Be that as it may, my hosts knew the flag and stopped. Not really because they wanted to pick up another Swiss, they thought I might need the company of a compatriot. I got out and spoke to him. He wasn't looking for a lift at all. He had just arrived and was making his way to the next town to find a new lift to the coast. I felt like the old couple had handed me a present I didn't really want but I didn't want to disappoint them, so I left with the Swiss. He'd been on the road a lot longer than me. This was his second Australia trip. He showed me where he was heading on my map. I think he was glad when I told him I was going the other way. We parted in the middle of a town. He went right, I went straight on.

Towns are the speed humps in hitchhiking. Cities are the curse. If you catch a lift, it usually ends in a town and if you are unlucky, it's on the wrong end and you have to walk all the way to the other end to continue your trip, because nobody picks you up right in the middle of town. That might be okay in a quaint little Swiss village but in Australia, even the crummiest little two-horse town is at least two miles long. I did a lot of walking, hitchhiking.

I stopped marking my progress on the map, names of towns and creeks. Actually, all of the creeks must have been named by the same people. Sandy Creek, Halfway Creek, Three, Four, Six, Eight, Nine, Ten Mile Creek. Australia had converted to metric not long before my trip. A lot of the road signs were still in miles and sausages were still in pounds. There were only two kinds: thick or thin. Beer, on the other hand, was numerous and came in packs or slabs. I had to open one of them during a ride I hitched in what would become my never to be realised forever car: a brand new Casino Blue Holden Sandman. It smelled like it had just come out of the showroom and rolled right into the pub next door. I had to crawl over a slab of beer when I got in the passenger seat. The driver was a well- dressed, cool-looking young guy and he put on the kind of music I like. Every now and then he made me open a stubby and hand it to him. I got a bit worried. He was on his way to a farm or whatever; I remember it had a sheep shearing shed. I assumed he was the owner because he told me he had to check the tallies, or the ringers or whatever one does if one owns a shearing shed. I almost didn't make it. I kept handing him stubbies, growing more and more worried. We stopped twice because he had to urinate on the roadside. At the second stop I pulled my pack from the back and walked off. He didn't say a thing, just watched me do it. A while later he pulled up right next to me and opened the passenger door. I can't remember what he said but it worked. I got back in and he didn't ask for any more beers.

When we got to the shed he asked me if I wanted to make a quick fifty bucks, helping with the wool press in the packing shed. I did. The lanoline and the wool fibres almost choked me to death. Every so often I would rush outside and put my head under the water tap. By evening I had fifty bucks and he offered me a ride back to his place and a bed for the night. I might be out of sync with my memory and for the life of me, I can't remember the city. I'm fairly sure the shearing shed was somewhere near Hamilton in Victoria, so I'm definitely out of sync. It took quite a while to get to his place and he was back asking for stubbies. When we arrived, it was dark and getting late. His wife or girlfriend opened the door and let him have it. She was just as cool looking as he was, even red hot angry. We both got an equal serve. He for being drunk and I for being the stray that followed him home. She won. He drove me to the station and I took a train to somewhere else. It came to me right now: he looked exactly like that cool dude in Hawaii Five-O.

In Mount Gambier I swam in the blue lake and hitched a lift from a student on his way to Port Macdonnell to meet up with a bunch of other students from Adelaide, holidaying in the small seaside town. Some of the students had found seasonal jobs on one of the cray boats in the harbour, putting out pots to catch rock lobsters. They took me out a few times and we rotated seventy pots and kept the undersized lobsters in hessian bags, ready to throw them overboard if the fisheries boat ever showed up. It never did. I shared a house with a three of the students. It was a dump with an outdoor dunny and a shower next to it. We kept the hessian bag in the shower and ate crayfish every night, except for Saturday, when the whole town crammed into a tiny pub, drank beer and put two dollars in a tin for steak and buffet salad. Earlier that year, Port Macdonnell had suffered a lot of storm and flood damage. The town looked like it was on its last legs but the lobster boats kept it going. Fishing was over by lunch, so everybody had a lot of time to play. I felt like I had trespassed into somebody else's Kombi years. Every now and then I hitched a ride with one of the students to get supplies from Mount Gambier. You couldn't buy anything in Port. On the way we would invariably stop at one of two houses that grew cannabis in the backyard. The mature plants were hanging all over the living room walls for drying. The students would stock up on weed and smoke it while driving. If I thought they were stoned, I'd take over driving. I wasn't smoking. I felt very old by now. It was time to look for an adult.

Not quite yet. I still had to pick up my guitar from Istvan. On the way to Melbourne I got a lift from a young woman. She was about my age. It took me a while to realise that she really had stopped for me. Lone young women just didn't pick up lone male hitchhikers. She was super pumped about it, too. She had just bought a plane ticket for her first trip abroad and she was bursting with happiness; she just had to share it with somebody, and that somebody turned out to be me. Go figure. She drove me all the way to Geelong and right into a camping ground. I stayed there for over a week and took the train into Flinders Street Station in Melbourne every morning and back in the afternoon. It felt a lot like commuting without a job to go to.

FOREVER DAY

On the first day in Melbourne, I went to the GPO and was directed to the counter that handled post restante or general delivery, as it was called there. I gave the guy behind the counter my name. He went to a back room and came back with devastating news: there was none. I was gutted. Heartbroken. I sat down in a square outside the Post Office, trying to figure out what could have gone wrong. I had faithfully sent letters to my parents. I just had to find out, so I went back in. The guy behind the counter either didn't recognize me or he didn't care. I got out my international drivers license and put it in front of him. This one he understood. He came back with a stack of letters. It was the happiest day of my trip. So far…. forever day was yet to come.

Ian had posted me a money order with an extra ten dollars interest added. In one of Mum's letters was a bank cheque from Dad. I had no problem cashing it in at the Commonwealth Bank down the road. It paid for two airline return tickets to Brisbane and Cairns in Queensland and Hobart in Tasmania. I was going to do Australia in six weeks if it killed me.

To find Istvan, I had to go through the Melbourne office of the Department of Emigration and Ethnic Affairs. I gave the woman who saw me all the details I had copied from Istvan's letter.

'Sorry, but I can't help you,' she said straight away. 'I don't know which agency processed your friend or where he ended up. Even if I knew, I could not tell you. We never give out that kind of information.'

'He asked me to come,' I said lamely. 'He has my guitar.'

'You'll just have to wait until he makes contact with you,' said the woman. 'It's up to him.'

FOREVER DAY

'I haven't heard from him and I don't have much time left.'

'Well, you'll have to find him yourself then.'

'How?'

'I can give you a list.'

'A list of what?'

'All the migrant hostels our department runs in Melbourne and surrounds.'

'And he'll be in one of them?'

'If he landed here and was processed here, most probably, yes.'

'And that's not classified information?'

'Migrant hostels are not prisons. People come and go, have family or friends calling in, prospective employers, health and social workers, the lot.'

She reached behind and pulled a small pamphlet from the shelf.

'Her you go,' she said.

I looked at the pamphlet. It was titled *'Welcome to Australia'*

'The list is on the back,' she said.

There were four entries under the heading *'Where You'll Stay'*

The woman reached across with her pen.

FOREVER DAY

'Springvale currently doesn't accept new intakes,' she said, crossing it out with her pen. 'These other two are handling mostly Vietnam migration after the fall of Saigon.'

'That leaves Nunawading,' I said.

'Bingo.'

Next day I took the Lilydale lane to Nunawading. The migrant hostel looked like a scene out of a World War 2 movie, with corrugated Nissen huts and Lancasters taking off to bomb the crap out of Berlin. That bit I added for illustration. Honestly, the place had all the vibe and charm of a world war two airfield, with a mess hall and crew quarters in even more Nissen huts.

I found Istvan in the mess hall. He didn't seem surprised to see me.

'How did you go?' he asked.

'I had a few hiccups but I made it.'

'You just missed Beka. She left the other day. Got a job in a bakery in Toorak through another Hungarian. She'll end up marrying a rich Australian, not a Swiss bum like you.'

'You mentioned that. Good for her', I said. 'Where is everybody else?

'Andris moved in with his brother, the others got jobs in Springvale. I have a job lined up as well. Panel beating. Another Hungarian. He's got a house and a business. I'll move in with him in a while. I'll give you his address.'

'Sounds like you have a proper Hungarian network going,' I said surprised.

FOREVER DAY

'Everybody has. The Italians, the Greeks, it's easier that way. I bet the Swiss have their own thing going.'

'I doubt that. We're not running away from the Russians or poverty. Level with me, Istvan. Was all that true?'

Istvan looked at me with the same grin Luke had flashed when he told me he'd rolled my car.

'You tell them what they want to hear. Most of us didn't really want to come here. We wanted to go to Canada and the USA but there were no places left. Have you come for your guitar?'

'Are you still playing?'

'Do you want to hear me play?'

'Sure.'

He took me to the sleeping quarters in another Nissen hut. It didn't look much different to my six berth cabin on the Marconi. My guitar stuck out of the top bunk just like the leg of the woman I had never met. Istvan grabbed it and played a tune. 'You're pretty good.'

'Better than you,' said Istvan. 'You suck.'

'So I've been told. Maybe you'll make it. Tell you what: keep the guitar. When you're a rock star I'll come and collect. Deal?'

'Are you still working on that book of yours?' asked Istvan.

'It's not a book. I just write down what I see. Like taking pictures. One day I might stick them in an album and that will be my book.'

FOREVER DAY

'Am I in it?'

'Sure.'

'Am I going to be the hero?'

'It won't be that kind of book.'

'Nobody wants to read about losers.'

'You're right. You'd better get your act together if you want to be my hero'

'Make me a rock star racing car driver. Where are you staying?'

'Camping ground in Geelong.'

'Where is that?'

'Out of the city. On the other side of the bay.

'You can stay here, if you like. Free food as well. Nobody cares. There are only five of us left in this hut.'

'I prefer to stay outside the city.'

'There is nothing there!'

'Space, Istvan. Lots and lots of it.'

'Not for me. Are you coming back?'

'To Australia? I don't know. I have a life to go back to.'

'What life? Your girlfriend kicked you out. You hated your job and you ran away. You're just the same as me.'

'I have a return ticket. You don't. That's the difference.'

11

Point of Exit

I'm convinced that all of Australia once was a lush paradise, but so was Mars. I crack up every time I read that people actually plan to settle there! There is no air on mars! Pick any spot in the middle of Australia and you're on Mars with all the air you'll ever need. It's a nicer shade of ochre than mars and it has a lot more life to boot. It's subtle, often insignificant and you have to look for it. Forget planes, trains and automobiles: when you hitchhike Australia, you walk her. Thanks to Dad's generosity I could hop on planes and take a bus, but as soon as I slung the pack on my shoulders, I was back amongst the roadkill, the rubbish and the beauty hiding underneath and beyond. There always is a beyond down under, after the next bend in the road, over the next hill. I never did Australia in six weeks. I did scratch the surface. I might have misunderstood some, judged some wrongly, but I was always and every bit of me, awed.

At first glance, the Galileo was an exact copy of the Marconi. She looked right beautiful sitting there like a white virgin bride on Circular Quay with the Sydney Harbor Bridge as backdrop. Up close, she was the prettier of the twins, and her cargo was a lot more to my liking.

My cabin was identical to the Marconi cabin. I shared with three other Swiss, old Walter, young Walter and Rudi, the remaining two berths stayed empty until New Zealand.

I chose first sitting in the dining room this time around, mainly to gain access to the soup. It's another Swiss thing. We always had soup as entree for dinner or lunch. Sadly, it didn't take long for another rumour to make the rounds. This time it was a gang of cockroaches reportedly circling the lid of the pot. Somebody really must have hated soup. It probably was the same guy that had first asked the powdered wine question. It too, had followed me on board the Galileo.

All the Italo-Australian families were still beating everybody else at Bingo and their kids still lorded over the swimming pool in their allotted time slot. There was still a first class that didn't mix but the mix of the other passengers was markedly different. There were no more migrants and a lot less old folks counting down the days to get back home. If the Marconi inbound was the tired old hag limping home, the Galileo outbound was the excited young sister on her way to do Europe and the world.

Once we cleared the harbour, the excitement toned down some, as we settled into the ship's routine. I found myself sitting in just about the exact same spot in the bar, right by the door between the inner and the outer decks. There were a lot more young people popping in and out of the bar, and a good portion of them were young single women. It certainly got the attention of our table with the two Walters, Rudi and the rest. To our amazement, the Swiss table had grown overnight to nine, which was about the same as having two percent of the population of my home town sitting in the bar of an Italian ship steaming towards New Zealand. That's where the other five Swiss were heading, spurred on by an invitation of the New Zealand government. They were all cashed up young farmers on their way to make milk and cheese under the long white cloud. They had travelled all the way from Genoa with the same mix of inbound travelers I had encountered on the Marconi. By now they were as horny as a herd of Swiss bulls, ready to jump on any young heifer coming their way. If you've never been on a ship you might not understand. It's the relentless vibration of the hull that gets to you.

FOREVER DAY

Amongst the newcomers in the bar were a bunch of young Australian women in their mid twenties. They were a close-knit group. The one that caught the farmers' attention was Merrilyn. She was lovely, dark haired with long eye lashes and a ready smile for everybody. The Swiss farmers were besotted by her. They had few words of English between them, so I ended up being the sucker who had to get their message across. Merrilyn had me tell them to get real. She was so far out of their league that it probably got lost in translation. She was a ballet dancer from Sydney on her first trip to Europe. She was all grace and style, with a steely determination to dance in Giselle with the Berlin Opera Ballet. The Swiss farmers left us, soon after.

Every night the band fired up their limited repertoire in the lounge. They weren't bad musicians, they just played crap music and they didn't have enough of that, either. They played the same song over and over again. If you want to see my head explode, just play *Kung Fu Fighting* for me! My forever girl likes to tease me by calling it our song. Yes, it happened. In the virgin hour of '76 with the only song the band ever played once, *Auld Lang Syne,* Janine caught my eye. To be honest, I had seen her before. She was part of Merrilyn's group. Maybe the light hadn't been right then, maybe my planets hadn't lined up, whatever the reason, here she was, slowly kissing her way from the lounge into the bar, wishing everybody a Happy New Year with a little peck. She wasn't very tall, fair to middling just like me. When she kissed a taller man, she stood on the tiptoe of one foot and slightly kicked up the other behind her, like Dorothy kissing the Tin Man in the Wizard of Oz. It was just so damn cute. She flashed the loveliest little smile I'd ever seen, with a mischievous sideways glance out of her big brown eyes. She wore a long dress with halter straps and bright red lipstick like Snow White in our play, and while I waited, last in line for her to find me, I knew, without a shadow of a doubt, that I was looking at my forever girl, all grown up.

No, the boat didn't rock and the earth didn't stop spinning, but I got my peck and one of her smiles. The year wasn't even one hour old and I was already running out of time. I had to grow up fast, if I wanted to catch up.

I had never really thought about the practicalities of a shipboard romance. How hard could it be? You kiss, you pash, you find a quiet corner and, if you're lucky, you get lucky. Thing is, there were no quiet corners on the Galileo. None whatsoever. Believe me: I checked. All the quiet corners were taken. On the top deck, under the mantle of darkness, there wasn't a square foot of spare deck to be had. The entire deck was a sea of moving blankets, pulled over couples mid-act. You'd have to be truly desperate to make love downwind from the ship's funnel, which spewed smoke and gritty little hard bits like the smokestack of a discount funeral home.

Staircases, too, made ideal little cubbyholes. You just had to hang your blanket off the side. I believe we first kissed right over one of those. Actually, I'm sure we did, downstairs, near my favourite spot on the poop deck and the wash of doom. I hadn't lured Janine there; we just bumped into each other, as you inevitably do on a ship that's only two hundred and fourteen metres long. That's around seven inches per passenger, if you do your maths.

If you're still with me after my first ever kiss, this was way better. You know, when you put your tongue over the two terminals of a battery, you get that little tingle, right? I don't know if people still do that these days. For us it was just a way of checking if there was any juice left. Anyway, kissing Janine was like that on high voltage. Touching her was like that. She made electric shadows under her finger tips. Deep Purple stole that line from Janine. If I'd had any sense, I would have rushed her right up to the Captain's and make him marry us on the spot. Turns out the Captain was busy courting Janine's sister. Fact. The sister might deny it, but we know better. It was the Captain of the crew, actually, not the Captain of the ship, but you couldn't tell them apart. Both were mature men pushing fifty, with that silver fox Latino lover look, packaged in a smart white Captain's uniform. For a girl growing up right next to a naval base with a thousand single sailors at her fingertips, she must have felt right at home.

I need to wind back a bit, so you understand. Janine and her sister, let's call her Lucy… or she'll probably stop talking to me, were part of that Australian young singles group who'd found each other on board. Janine was a Catholic primary school teacher; Lucy, a hairdresser. They lived with their parents in a weatherboard right next door to the naval base HMAS Cerberus on the Western Port Peninsula. Their dad was a NCO shipwright in the Australian Navy; their mum, a seamstress on base. Short of growing up on a battle cruiser, you couldn't get more naval than that. You also couldn't get more Catholic than that. I only mention it because I don't want you to get the wrong impression. Janine and Lucy might have danced and charmed an entire naval base, but behind that beautifully wicked smile were always the moral compass and the guilt of a Good Catholic Girl. Quite apart from that, the sailors on base treated women with far more respect and courtesy than the typical city nightclub crowd ever did.

The sisters had caught the travelling bug visiting their brother, who was teaching English at the RAAF base Butterworth on the Malaysian mainland near Penang. Europe was their next joint adventure. It was going to be Lucy's last hurrah before settling down. She was pushing thirty. Janine was three years younger and had made up her mind to become a career teacher. Tough luck to both of them! Lucy ran into the Captain of the crew while Janine melted right into Swiss chocolate.

According to Lucy, the Captain of the crew affair was pure conjecture of two lovestruck romantics, watching the world through rose-coloured glasses. I beg to differ. She shared a double with Janine but she was never there, which would have been great news for us, if she hadn't taken the key with her to the Captain's cabin, where nothing ever happened. Beautiful blond Lucy with the suave Italian gray fox, having tea and biscuits in his cabin in an all-nighter. Not even the Pope would buy that story. I only met the Captain once. Janine and I were mid-kiss, mid-cuddle, parked in front of the locked cabin door. Or maybe it was the other way round, maybe they came out. Whatever. I can't recall if we spoke, but I distinctly remember the Captain giving me a once-over. Disapproving. Like I was the bum on deck.

When the Australian girls finally landed in Genoa, Lucy made them walk all the way to an apartment block just to look up at the Captain's flat on the third floor. I would've loved to be there, knocked on the door, maybe. They didn't. After touring Europe, Lucy went back to Australia and married an Australian shipwright who could neither swim nor float. Water under the Galileo.

New Zealand to Fiji was just a hop and a skip. I frankly don't know why we stopped there. We had only hours, no time to learn anything about the country and its many islands, other than to bring an umbrella. It was the wet season. It was hot. It poured rain for a bit, then back to hot and sunny, and before you dried out, the next load of rain hit. The girls took a sightseeing bus trip. I watched them leave and started dreading my own departure.

FOREVER DAY

We stopped over in Tahiti next and checked out the Gauguin museum. I went with the boys; Janine with the girls, Lucy dined with the Captain in a fancy restaurant up on one of the hills behind the harbour. The sly fox probably had a season ticket. There weren't enough seats on the buses so everybody else had to hitch rides in cars for a fare. The locals must have used it to make some money on the side. I think you could bargain but it was dirt cheap anyway. Janine and a couple of the other girls hitched a ride with some young fellows, after their bus driver called it a day halfway through the trip back. They made it close to the ship when the young fellows turned into the driveway of a residence. They had been drinking and probably thought it was party time. The girls jumped out of the car and ran all the way back to the ship. I learned about the near miss in the evening and started worrying some more.

There was a lot of water between Tahiti and Acapulco and my clock was slowly winding down. When I was not with Janine, I left the bar and slept in my cabin and ate lunch in the dining room, like normal people do. Janine and I had talked enough for me to realise that a life with her was only going to happen on day shift, with firm ground under our feet, and it had to be by my choice, not her ultimatum. I mean, we were still joking around and flirting and doing our own thing with our own groups, but when we were together alone, we told each other that's where we wanted to be, and I swore to myself, that I wouldn't leave this boat without telling her how I felt and that she'd better get ready to have our babies. Once bitten, twice shy.

And then we were in Acapulco. Janine and her gang went up the hill to visit the Chapel of Peace, home to the world's most famous cross. Lucy took a break from dining with the Captain and tagged along, no doubt to confess the thing that never happened. I

FOREVER DAY

followed the boys into town in search of authentic Mexican food. We ended up in a great big shed of a place, with a band on stage and the kitchen in the dining room: vats of food on sandstone tables, hand-painted tiles, and great big lumps of smoked bacon hanging from the rafters. Bottles of wine and beer lined a sideboard. All the beer bottles had their caps removed, replaced with folded white paper napkins. I asked one of the diners why. He said it was for hygiene. I get it, but it still doesn't make sense to me. It tasted okay. So did the food. So did everything else. The three piece band was loud and very Mexican. No bloody sombreros and false moustaches. Just three old guys belting out a tune. We were seated right below them. At one stage, they played a soft slow number and the singer bent over the stage, singing right into old Walter's face. I have to tell you that old Walter was what is often called a slight man, short with fine features. He also had a limp but you only noticed if you walked with him. He was smart as a whip, educated at the most prestigious of Zurich universities with a degree in architecture and urban design. He once put a sketch of a skyscraper on my notepad. I should have framed and sold it to the Guggenheim Museum. Sitting in this Mexican joint, with the singer clearly serenading him, Walter didn't flinch. At the end of the song, everybody clapped and Walter just nodded his appreciation. He wasn't gay, if that's what you think. I lost him in Curacao but later on, back in Switzerland, I got in touch with him. He had a rough time, falling for a Kiwi that soon after dumped him. That's what cruising on ships does to you.

Young Walter on the other hand, was the exact opposite of old Walter. I know he was Swiss because he spoke Swiss German, but he certainly didn't look it. He fitted like a glove into our current surrounds. I guess he was a very good looking guy, if you go for that Spanish dark brood. Later in Cristobal, we were drinking in what clearly was a whore house, one of the girls came up to him and asked him how much. He told her, how much do you pay me? That kind of guy, but he was fun.

Rudi was the fourth wheel on our Swiss wagon, and true to his name, he knew no shame. Tougher than the entire Italian night crew of Lloyd Triestino put together, he was another little guy, even smaller than old Walter, but built like a brick. Buff, toned, and stitched together from old fractures, he'd broken every bone in his body at least once. By day, he fixed forklifts. By choice, he raced 1000cc motorcycles, and judging by the scars, he fell off them as often as he stayed on. When I asked him if the prize money made it all worth it, he couldn't stop laughing. In his last race he was placed third and won a can of motor oil. I was really impressed by his dedication. Breaking that many bones for your true love. With the human kind of love he was a lot less engaged. Rude. Once Margot sat at our table and got talking to him. I don't know what it was all about, but at one stage he got up and grabbed his balls and told her: 'I know what you want.' It's sad and funny if you can picture Margot. She was one of Janine's gang, around thirty, always dressed in what I call arty flowing gowns, with bits hanging off the side. She taught art at a high school and she was going to schlep her Australian friends around every ruin, every sculpture and every framed painting in Europe, and she could tell them everything there was to know about it. Rude Rudi wasn't making any friends but later on, in Cristobal, he was happy to pay for five minutes of a woman's attention.

Our day in Acapulco was the only stopover all of us truly enjoyed. We met up with the girls back on board, and they told us about their day in yet another church, where people milled about eating and drinking in one great big fiesta, while the priest tried to hold mass in a far corner. Out of the blue, I said: 'I couldn't marry a Catholic.'

FOREVER DAY

'Who asked you?' said Janine.

Of all the dumb things I've said, this one takes the cake. No clue where it came from. I wasn't even religious. I never, ever asked anybody what religion he or she was. Until now, it hadn't quite registered that Janine was, in fact, a devout believer, and once I knew her better, I could see that she had grown up in a world different to mine, where school kids called each other names because they went to schools with different denominations. The Swiss had fought wars for hundreds of years for the very same reason until, one day; they stopped and ate bready milky soup together. By the time I came along, the Catholic and Protestant bashing was well and truly done, and I was not going to start it up once more. I somehow got out of it. I mean, the proof is in the pudding. I married a Catholic in a Catholic church. But if you think that settled it, think again. My sweet forever woman knows how to twist a knife.

Cristobal is the harbour that goes with the Panama Canal. It was a dump. I don't think any tourist ship would have stopped there if it wasn't for supplies. I've never been back so I can only tell you what I saw then. Before we debarked into the night, we were warned not to wear any jewellery and to stay on the main stretch under the lights. It's the kind of tourist advice you don't want to hear when visiting a place. I think only a few of us actually ventured out. I went with young Walter and Rudi. The main stretch was just a short road with cops standing guard on both sides. There wasn't much to see or do. A few shops were open, including a drug shop that sold every prescription drug you can think of, freely available over the counter.

We went into a bar that turned out to be a whore house. There were a lot of older German guys from a merchant ship there, sweating and drinking beer, waiting for their heartbeat to settle before they went for another ride with one of the Columbian girls. It was packed, on both sides of the isle. The girls were plentiful, young and pretty and they'd come out into the bar and try to get you to follow them into one of the cubicles at the back. Young Walter did his how-much-do-you-pay-me spiel; I said I had no money and Rudi grabbed a towel from the attendant by the doorway and followed a girl that looked to be about twelve years old. He was back before we finished our beers. We didn't ask. We left but Rudi turned back for more. No amount of going back was going to give him anything he'd paid for.

Young Walter and I walked into the dark. There were no more street lights. We spotted a takeaway with the lights on. There were some young locals in there, eating chicken and chips. They came over and asked us if we wanted to buy some weed. I declined but young Walter was interested. They told us to follow them down the road. After a minute or two they disappeared behind a stone wall. We heard somebody running and shouting, and took off ourselves, heading back towards the lights. We didn't get far. A cop car stopped us and they made us hop in and transported us back to the stretch we were told not to leave.

And then, much too early for my liking, we reached Curacao. We must have docked on the poor side of town. There were no other ships around us. A bit further downtown, there were rows of large cruise ships, five stories high or more. Everybody went shopping. The whole place was just one big shopping mall, full of Americans buying up grog, jewellery, perfume and whatever else was duty free. Janine and I found a place in a park to say our goodbyes. We were both a little sad but full of confidence that we would soon be together again. I wanted her to have a piece of me, so I gave her the coin with the chain I wore around my neck. She gave me a picture of herself. I told her I was going to see the ship off. We kissed goodbye and she ducked into the next shop to buy a new watch to start counting the hours.

The Galileo departed in the late afternoon. I made my way to the dock. On the way, I bought a banana I thought I'd eat while waiting for the ship to make its way out to sea. When I got there, the ship was nearly ready to go. The dockside was deserted, just two or three guys pulling ropes from the bollards. No one else was waving goodbye.

Up on the ship, everyone I cared about had lined the railing three stories above me. They shouted encouragement, but it was hard to hear. The ship began to move, tugged gently away from the dock. Someone tossed an orange down from above, then another. I spotted Janine's cat-print dress fluttering in the wind. I felt tiny, utterly insignificant, as the big ship picked up speed and glided past. I waved once more and turned to leave.

One of the port workers handed me the two oranges from the dock and pointed at the banana in my hand.

'Platano,' he said with a big grin. 'No eating. Cooking.'

In one of the oranges I found a folded five dollar bill, in the other two joints wrapped in plastic. I put the five dollars towards drinks in a bar that night. I felt pretty good by then. In keeping with the locals, I drank Curacao, a sweet liquor I normally wouldn't touch. I had one or two in blue, one orange and one red. They all tasted the same and left me with a headache.

The next morning, I went down to the pier where the small boats from Venezuela tied up to sell fresh fruit and vegetables. I figured I might hitch a ride with one of them. Venezuela was only forty miles across the Caribbean Sea. I tried a few boats, but nobody wanted to take me. So I booked a flight for the following morning.

I hadn't smoked the two joints. I was well and truly over it, but I thought Jeampi might appreciate them. They were wrapped tight in plastic. I opened the toothpaste tube from the back and slid them inside. At the airport, just before boarding, I had second thoughts and tossed the tube in a bin. Just as well. They strip-searched me in Caracas and went through everything in my pack. I was clean.

Midnight Express wouldn't be made for another two years, but I could've starred in the Venezuelan version.

I was planning to give you a rundown of my stay, but I won't. It's just too sad. Not then, now. While working on this chapter, I finally managed to reach my old friend, someone I hadn't seen in nearly fifty years. Turns out he was back in Switzerland. His lovely, beautiful wife, Marines, had died of breast cancer. My godson Werner was killed in a car crash. And Venezuela, the country he had chosen and loved, Venezuela was, and still is, in utter chaos, ruined and run by criminal cartels of drug dealers.

After all those years, after building a family and a successful business, Jeampi was forced to sell everything and return to where he came from.

I can't think of anything more heartbreaking.

12

Ten finger job

Back in Switzerland I waited for Janine, who was by then working her way towards Scotland, of all places. She never felt a drop of rain and she married a fellow traveller in a blacksmith shop in Gretna Green for fun. I later showed her fake marriage certificate to Dad and had him utterly confused.

I put the picture of Janine on my bedside table and kissed her good morning and good night, every day. She was worth waiting for. She was beautiful, she was smart, and she came with an entire continent. I was determined to make it all mine.

Before I started looking for a job, I typed out my handwritten travelling notes on a Hermes portable. I'm Ritchie Blackmore on a typewriter. Ten fingers, Jimi! I never really worried too much about getting the spelling right, so I had it done in a week. It was in German and I titled it *'Nothing moves here except the sun'*. I sent the manuscript to a publisher and got my first pink slip within another week, which, honestly, was incredibly fast. It was a pink slip, but not quite. The publisher liked the story so much he replied immediately, just to give me time to submit it to another house, Sauerländer, who happened to be looking for new authors right then.

They accepted my story. So before I even started looking for a paying job, I had one that didn't pay.

The paying job I found was in accounting with a firm that manufactured wood fired heaters and custom built stone and metal fireplaces. I went to the hairdresser and got myself a sharp new haircut. With Janine still on the road, I told them it probably was going to be a temporary position. They were happy with it. All they wanted me for was to bring their accounts receivable up to scratch. They had amassed an amazingly large backlog of overdue accounts in various stages of debt recovery. I sorted out the most pressing ones that had stalled for months and years.

Fireplaces in Switzerland are like swimming pools in Australia. You buy one to warm up or cool down, or you install a great big whopper just to show off. Not surprisingly, those were the ones people didn't pay for.

I picked the longest-running dispute first. We'd made numerous attempts to settle. The owner refused to pay because of a small flaw in the travertine stone surrounding his fireplace.

Travertine is porous. It has to be treated and filled. Some stones come with natural holes that need a bit more filler. This entire dispute was over one of those spots, no bigger than a fifty-cent piece.

I visited the owner at his home and tried to offer a reasonable deduction for the flaw. He wouldn't listen. He was a fidgety kind of guy. I knew from the records that he worked as a pilot for Swissair. I began to really worry about how deeply upset he was, all because of a small impurity in the stone.

I pictured him flying a plane with two hundred and fifty passengers at thirty thousand feet, worrying about the filled hole in his fireplace surround. What if he was piloting the very plane Janine was flying home in?

I tried to reason with him. Told him I was just doing my job, and that I could spend hours, even days or weeks on it, and still get paid. He, on the other hand, had to take time off and drive all the way home. I suggested he get a lawyer, someone who'd love to spend long, billable hours with me. All it did was make him more likely to crash a plane.

I took the case to the Office of the Lay Justice, a uniquely Swiss system to settle claims outside the main courts. Lay justices often were retired judges or notary publics or similar dignified types. The LJ ordered an on-site inspection. He showed up with his staff. I waited for them by the door.

The pilot insisted we take our shoes off before entering the house. We stood in a carpeted hall with wide steps leading upstairs to where the fireplace was. The LJ was an old retired judge with arthritic knees. He groaned when he bent down, trying to get his shoes off. I bent over and did it for him. It was just an automatic reaction of a young man helping his elder. The LJ groaned some more when we climbed up plush steps leading to the fireplace awaiting judgment.

'Where is it?' the judge asked.

The pilot pointed to the spot in the fireplace surround. The judge got closer, took his glasses off and wiped his eyes with the back of his hand, before putting the glasses back on.

'Where?'

'Right here!'

The judge stepped up to the spot and bent over as much as he could.

'I still can't see it!'

I could milk this for all its worth but you already know how it ended. Judgment for the plaintiff. I still let the pilot take six hundred francs off the bill, double the amount the company had offered him two years ago. If you're a passenger in his plane, you might owe me your life.

It was my first job for the company. I wasn't exactly thrilled about it, mostly because I couldn't understand why anyone would fuss so much over something so trivial. But most of the cases that followed? I genuinely enjoyed them. There was a certain satisfaction in making some tight-ass rich bastard cough up for a fireplace big enough to roast a pig.

I did well. Not because I was some hot-shot, Perry Mason-style legal eagle, but because I always tried to avoid conflict. I always tried to settle the cases, even the ones I could easily have won. If you think about it, that's what life is all about. Compromise.

Finally, Janine showed up. I picked her up from the airport in Dad's better car. She had changed her hairdo as well. She looked very smart and even more grown up. I took her home to my parents' new place and she was my deer in the meadows, my spring field of rose and buttercup, charged like a thunderstorm, wired to a million watts.

It was to be our last time in the new place. Dad was going to rent it out. He had bought another, much bigger place, right by the new road in the town centre, opposite where the old pub had stood. When I came home from South America, they had already moved in. It was an ancient three storey mansion, built by a Major Honegger in the 18th century. Locally it was known as the Honegger house. The ground floor and the first floor were in good condition, all the upstairs rooms where the servant's quarters used to be, were not fit for living. It still had the wires from the old servant's bell system hanging on the walls.

FOREVER DAY

Dad had bought a digger he could hook up to his tractor. He dug up the old concrete swimming pool and pulled down the stables. He was going to build a new pub right there. Janine and I moved into our newly refurbished room on the first floor. I had just started my new job, so I couldn't take much time off. I didn't like leaving her home alone, but at least she had my family for company. I could see that she was getting itchy feet. She missed home and she had a job to go back to.

Her sister came over from England for a visit. Dad lent them his good car and they took off to tour Switzerland. After they came back, Lucy left for England; Janine waited for me at my parents' place to come home for lunch and dinner. In our free time we made love and I showed her around and showed her off to my friends. None of them spoke English well enough for any meaningful conversation, but we could still eat and drink and have fun. We could have just stayed that way forever. Janine was smart; she'd pick up German in no time. I never asked her, but we knew where we were heading. Back to Australia, into the church and out bush. My immigration application was already with the Australian Embassy in Bern. My compass was set. So was Janine's. Her job was waiting, so were her parents and friends; it was time for her to go home. Off she went once more on a plane back home. We started writing letters to each other. For a while she worried that she had returned pregnant but it turned out to be a false alarm.

My publisher, Sauerländer, arranged a meeting with the editor, Irana Bodlakova at the publisher's place of business in the city of Aarau. It had to be on a Saturday because of work, mine and theirs.

FOREVER DAY

'I thought that's what you'd look like,' she said, when we first met. I really should have asked her how she had figured that out, but I was a bit overawed right then. She was much older than me but kind of cool and arty-looking, like Margot from the ship. When I called her Mrs. Bodlakova, she insisted on first names. In Switzerland that's close to a first date.

Irana showed me around the business. It was housed in a beautiful old place, much bigger than I had thought. They were publishers and contract printers. Their publishing arm was mainly children's books. I believe they printed the best quality illustrated children's books anywhere in Europe at that time. I was very impressed.

Irana showed me into her office and we sat down. She picked up a folder with my manuscript in it. When she opened it, I stared at a sea of red ink. I couldn't help but cracking up.

Irana looked at me wistfully.

'You know what?' she asked, closing my folder. 'Let's do this somewhere else.'

I followed her down the road into town and into a pub. It smelled of old wood and onions, a lot better than her office. Irana paused at the bar.

'Go and find us a table,' she said 'What are you having?'

'I'll have what you're having.'

She smiled and shook her head but she said nothing.

Irana came over to the table I had chosen. She put a glass of milk in front of me.

FOREVER DAY

'Milk?'

'You ordered it.'

'Very funny.'

She opened the folder and took out my manuscript.

'Do you want to do this now?'

'Not really.'

'So what do you want me to do?'

'Can you please just fix it?'

'It's got your name on it. I usually don't write for authors.'

'I'll buy you lunch.'

Irana gave me a sly look.

'You're older than you look.'

'I can smell them cooking. I'm hungry.'

'Okay. They do a very good lunch here. Go for menu one. It's the one the chef spends some time with. Menu two is always Wiener schnitzel with chips and peas. I still want to talk about your manuscript.'

Lunch arrived in no time. It was Saturday; there weren't that many diners in the restaurant. I could picture this place on a weekday, filled with workers on their lunch break, and the kitchen humming in the background. It always reminded me of home.

We talked a bit while we ate lunch. Irana told me that my book would have a print run of one thousand copies. It was the publisher's break-even number.

'If you reach it, we might consider a second submission. If you don't, you'll die.'

'Sounds harsh.'

'It's a new line for us. Upcoming authors. We call it *New Texts*. You're the fourth one in line. So far we've made no money at all.'

'You're still paying me? How much do I get?'

'Ten percent of the retail price for every hard copy sold. Five to seven percent for paperbacks, half that for third party translations. We'll give you an advance of five hundred, the balance of the royalties we'll pay half-yearly.'

'I make more than that in a week, and I don't have to wait half a year to get paid.'

Irana looked at me and smiled.

'It's a tough gig, kiddo! But you already knew that, right?'

'The weirdo reporter?'

She didn't answer.

'What made you send us the manuscript?' she asked instead.

'I really don't know. I just thought it would be nice to have my story in a book that I could hand on to my friends. And maybe I hoped I could beat the odds. I'm going back to Australia and if I can make some money writing, that would be a bonus.'

FOREVER DAY

'It's a lottery. You might still make it. Do you know why I accepted your story?'

'No idea. Because you liked it?'

'Yes, but I like a lot of the stories I look at every day. I picked yours because you don't try to sound like a writer. That's rare. It makes you real. That's why I said I knew what you looked like.'

'I make up stuff.'

Irana laughed. 'I know you do,' she said, 'but there is a grain of truth in every sentence. You keep that up and you'll get better. But for fuck's sake: check your spelling.'

I started to enjoy my new paid job. Apart from the sheer satisfaction of making some tight-ass rich guy cough up for work my employer had already paid decent men to do, it also came with generous helpings of me-time.

Most of our work was in Zurich canton. Clean, local, and paid for. But interstate debtors? They figured red tape would scare us off. Switzerland is just a speck of a country, the size of a postage stamp on a postcard with scenic views; you can literally traverse it in a matter of hours. Yet it has half as many individual states as the United States of America, each with its own spoken dialect, its own tax code, and a voting system so local they hold referendums on whether a teacher is allowed to teach. Not surprisingly, they also had their own rules for how you could make their citizens pay for an unpaid fireplace; one the owners had hoped would keep them warm for the price of a single log of wood. Not if I had my way.

FOREVER DAY

Given my limited experience with the Australian bureaucracy, I was expecting a smooth passage for my visa application. I still can't believe how incredibly stupid I was.

I know you're bursting with expectation to hear my story unfold, but please allow me to jump ahead a couple of decades, to the moment I had to deal with the Australian champion of the world's bureaucracies: Centrelink. Invented by Cane and Abel, perfected by William Tell and Erich Honecker with help from the Stasi in the GDR, it's the absolute and undisputed gem of Australian call-waiting bureaucracy, easily outdoing Telstra, Optus, and Medicare combined.

I don't really need to illustrate it for my fellow Australians, who've spent a good part of their lives on hold with them. Still, for the rest of you, and for my own peace of mind, I just have to get this off my chest.

By that time, our children had started university. Surprise, though not for us. They were planned. We had three by then.

Anyway, our middle child, Denise, was in a car accident. You guessed it: a gravel truck in a hurry rear-ended her on the on-ramp and shoved her car onto the median strip of a busy highway, clipping a third vehicle on the way. Rear-end accidents and luck run in the family.

The car was a write-off, but she wasn't hurt. Just to be sure, Janine took her to the family doctor, who thought she was fine. However, because the consult was the result of an accident, the doctor made Janine fill out a multi-page form to claim back the forty dollar fee.

We didn't hold our breath. We thought the form had melted right into the great big bucket of swill that feeds bureaucracies the world over. But it hadn't. Months later, the Compulsory Third Party Insurance sent us a settlement proposal. Two thousand dollars if we let them off the hook.

Denise was over the moon. She was studying towards her Bachelor of Education degree and working part-time at the cash register in Coles. She couldn't sign fast enough.

I bought her a new old car from a mate of mine. It was a beauty: 1971 Holden Kingswood with a near-perfect original paint job and very low mileage.

A bit later, Denise drove Mum to church one Sunday evening. While they were at mass, the Kingswood got stolen. I mean, what kind of lowlife steals a Kingswood from a church parking lot?

The car was registered in my name. Next morning, before I could even report it stolen, I got a call from the local police telling me my car was on fire up in the hills behind town.

They said, and I quote: 'You have to come and get it. It's an environmental hazard.' They gave me the address. I think it was *Lover's Lane* near Fernvale, or close to it.

Sure enough, there was the Kingswood, roasting away in the middle of an acre of burning scrub and dry grass. I thought the cops would be there in force, waiting for the fire brigade to arrive. No such luck. They hadn't called anybody but me. My car, my problem.

I called triple zero, and they alerted the Country Fire Authority, which eventually appeared with a small truck manned by half a dozen volunteers. One of them came up to me and asked, and I quote: 'Did you light it?'

'Are you crazy? It's my car. Somebody stole it and set it alight. The cops rang me, so I came.'

'We get that quite a bit up here.'

'Aren't you going to do something about it? Put out the fire?'

'Too late for the car. The fire will run out of fuel all by itself.'

He hopped back into the truck, and before they took off, he called out: 'You'll have to remove the car. It's an environmental hazard.'

My brother-in-law was friends with a backyard mechanic up in the hills. He graciously removed the environmental hazard and put it in the field behind his own place.

By about that time, Centrelink swung into action. The insurance company had woken up the beast and it came for us by letter, asking why we had failed to declare the two thousand dollars compensation. Denise was on a modest Austudy Allowance. She had faithfully reported her meagre income from her checkout job at Coles. None of us had realised that rear-end collision compensation should have been reported as well. Fair enough, we apologised for the oversight and filled out the appropriate form.

That form led to another form, and eventually a cut in her allowance.

Our eldest daughter, Corinne, was also studying toward a veterinary science degree. She too was on Austudy. Because the cut in one sibling's allowance caused whatever ripple effect in whatever other department, I was told my income had changed. I was self-employed, so I should have known. I didn't have a clue what it was all about.

FOREVER DAY

I could bore the socks off you with an explanation, but I won't. The long and short of it was: I had to fill out another sixty-four-page actual means assessment form.

I sent it in. Nothing happened

When I enquired, they couldn't find it. I hadn't made a copy, so I did it all again, made a copy, and took the original to Centrelink, asking for a confirmation-of-lodgment stamp.

Nothing happened. My form was nowhere to be found and they stopped all payments.

I asked for an interview and took Janine for company, mainly to keep me from committing mass murder. Turns out it was the other way round. I was Mister Cool and Reasonable; she stormed out and told everyone waiting in the mile-long queue outside that they were just wasting their time.

I wasn't. I had an epiphany. The case manager looked like every other Australian. Outside his job, he probably hated Centrelink as much as the rest of us.

I asked him calmly what exactly he needed from me to get my daughters back on Austudy; not with another form, but what he wanted to see on that form. He told me. And that solved the problem.

For a while.

By the time our youngest, Michael, entered the fray, Centrelink was run by politicians and computers. The beast had grown bigger teeth and lost all of its humanity. I had to fight it through the Administrative Appeals Tribunal and appeal the decision in court. My hair turned grey, but I won.

FOREVER DAY

I hadn't learned any of this when I was waiting for my visa back in '76, turning into '77. My advance arrived, and I put it towards two top-notch fondue sets, one for cheese, the other for Fondue Bourguignonne, where you cook little choice bits of meat in a pot full of hot oil and eat them with all sorts of vegetables and sauces.

Dad never ate it with us. He reckoned it was like feeding strawberries to an elephant. He preferred his meat barbequed in one piece.

Finally, the Australian Embassy in Bern stirred and invited me for an interview. I had the use of a company car by now, so the Australian Embassy was now officially on my list of unpaid fireplaces as well.

The young visa processing officer who interviewed me looked a lot like Janine. Same hair, same stature, same niceness, even similar dress. And like Janine, she was from Victoria too.

I didn't seriously hit on her, she wore a ring, but with so much Janine in another attractive Australian woman, I guess I flirted a bit. After five months of waiting, I was just as horny, clumsy, and dumb as the herd of Swiss bulls on the Galileo with Merrilyn.

I made her smile when I asked where she was from and what had brought her to Switzerland, but I put my foot in it soon enough.

The question was: 'Can you state the reason why you want to settle in Victoria?'

'Because of the beautiful Victorian girls.'

First strike. Maybe I should not have used the plural.

FOREVER DAY

'How do you intend to support yourself in Australia?'

'I'll get myself a job.'

'What job? Have you made any contacts regarding paid employment in Australia?'

'It's a bit hard applying from here.'

'You state your qualifications as Notary Public. That's not on our list of professions eligible for a skilled migration visa. Do you have any other qualifications?'

Strike two. On second thoughts, she didn't look that much like Janine.

'You can apply for a partner visa, subclass 820. It'll be temporary for two years. After that, if you're still in Australia, you'll be granted an 801 visa. Or you can apply for a prospective marriage visa -subclass 300, valid for nine months, which then converts to a 309 visa, and eventually a class 100 visa after two years.

Alternatively, you can apply for a Significant Investor visa - subclass C188, which requires an investment of five million dollars or more, held for at least four years. I assume that doesn't apply to you?'

'Wow!'

'What if I'm running away from the oppressive Swiss government and forced military service? Is there a visa class for that?'

'You don't have a record, do you? Be honest. We'll check. You'll also have to pass a medical before we can grant you a visa.'

FOREVER DAY

Strike three.

'What'll it be? 820 or 300?'

By now my head was spinning. All I could think of was the five million entry fee. That equalled ten thousand book advances or fifty years of hard labour at my current wage.

'Do you want me to give you your options once more?' she asked kindly. I could see that she didn't like to inflict pain.

'What would you do?' I asked. 'You're married, right?'

'I don't know what that has to do with your application.'

'So you are married. What would you do if you were here and your husband was in Australia? What would you do?'

'He is, actually. Take the 820. It will give you two years to regret your decision before we kick you out.'

I felt a lot better once I was in the car heading home. Things were finally in motion.

I hit the A1 motorway on the outskirts of Bern and noticed a hitchhiker on the on-ramp. I slowed down. To my utter amazement, he had the Australian flag on his backpack. I would've stopped anyway, but how creepy was that?

He was young me, asked where I was going, and I invited him to stay at my parents' house. They had plenty of spare rooms. He was thrilled to bits.

His name was Mark, and he was from New Zealand.

Potato, potahto.

FOREVER DAY

You know, I never asked him what he did for a living. Not that I cared. He was just young Mark from New Zealand.

We had a couple of spare rooms on the second floor and were in the process of getting two more ready, stuffed full of old furniture left behind by the previous owners. Mark was right into it. He cleaned those rooms for my parents, and when he was done, he cleaned out the outside shed and the coal cellar as well. He filled four big skips in as many days.

Dad would've adopted him in a flash, but Mark already had parents, they were on their way over to Switzerland. After a week or so, they finally arrived in Zurich and claimed their son back.

The waiting slowly got to me. I could feel it in the music I listened to. Jimi and Ritchie stayed tucked away in their record sleeves; instead, I put on the Eagles and Steely Dan. It's a mood thing.

I still had a few old friends around, but they were married, hitched, or just happy having the sex or the love, I wasn't getting.

I got bored waiting. And for me, that meant writing some more. In the lone evenings, instead of hitting the city, I hit my Hermes portable. I wrote short stories for a teen magazine called *Team*. They lapped it up. I started another novel, just in case Sauerländer didn't kill me off. I wrote a few pieces for the Press Agency Dukas in Zurich. I never met anyone from their organisation, but I always pictured it as a small one-room office somewhere in downtown Zurich: a desk, a fax, a coffee machine, and a mature woman quietly filing my words away.

They always paid me for anything that got picked up.

FOREVER DAY

I had to take another fireplace-debtor-collecting trip to Bern, this time to do my medical for the Australian Embassy. Their prescribed medical examiner was probably the oldest Swiss practitioner alive. Remember those days at school, when the doctor and his wife showed up in primary school to check our testicles, that was him.

The wife would sit outside and register your name. You'd go into the examining room, drop your pants, and the doctor would make you put your hands over your mouth and cough while inspecting your lower regions, then call out to his wife: 'No break.' I don't really know what that meant. I guess they were looking for hernias.

He made me do just that. Then he checked my lungs and every other organ that could pose a liability to the Australian government. No break. Clean as a whistle. Ready to melt Swiss cheese into the Great Australian Pie.

You guessed it: one more holdup. I knew that Janine would have to sign a statutory declaration to look after her poor, unqualified bum of a husband-to-be for at least two years. What I didn't know was that sending out the necessary paper for her to sign, required my application to be married to my medical, somewhere in a dark corner of the embassy.

That marriage then produced a statutory declaration form, flown by diplomatic bag to Canberra, sent by pouch to Melbourne, delivered by mail to Janine, signed in the presence of a JP, returned to sender, pouch, diplomatic bag, Australian Embassy, requesting my passport, stamping it, and returning it by registered mail- and Glory, Hallelujah, I was cleared for takeoff.

FOREVER DAY

Chickens can hatch an egg in three weeks. The birth of my visa took the best part of nine months. We could have celebrated the birth of our firstborn right there and then.

13

Haste to the Wedding

Janine picked me up from Tullamarine Airport at 5 a.m., in early August 1977. It was winter, cold and dark outside. The heater in her car was broken. Insert, insert, should have bought a Kingswood. She was extremely nervous, like she was on a first date with a complete stranger.

We reached Frankston by sun-up. She stopped at a milkbar to buy a box of matches. I realised she was stalling for time, but I didn't know why. The guy in the milkbar had the hot plate going for his own breakfast, so Janine ordered a couple of hamburgers with the lot. Best breakfast I've ever had.

By now I was sure Janine was stalling, and I asked her why.

'Just, you know… my parents' house is nothing like your parents' place. Much smaller.'

'Do you think I care?'

'I just don't want you to be disappointed. We'll get our own place soon. Right?'

'It's me, Janine. The guy from the ship. Remember?'

'Yeah, I know. I'm just nervous, that's all.'

'You'll be fine. Let's get it over with.'

That's why I like going to pubs. I'm welcome. Nobody asks me why I'm there. Nobody apologises for the bad light, or the smell, or the furniture. I'm there to pick up a drink, or food, or company. If Janine had grown up in a pub, she'd understand. I was here to pick up Janine. That's all.

Half an hour later, we drove into Crib Point. Janine slowed right down to give me a chance to let it all sink in. This was the town she'd grown up in. The two-room schoolhouse up the hill, where she still taught. The guard box at the entry to HMS Cerberus, where she'd watched movies and danced. The butcher, the post office, the milkbar; Cellars, the corner shop, where she'd asked for lollies on her fifth birthday and worked the counter for spending money as an adult.

She could tell me who lived in every house along the way to her parents' place, and she knew the owner of every dog that roamed the streets.

It brought back memories of my parents' very first place, when I was just tall enough to clear the front gate, running out of the house to marvel at a passing car on a dusty road.

Janine's town was that kind of place: with crooked power poles and power lines sagging from house to house; footpaths with concrete slabs that never quite met; bitumen roads that never quite hardened; and life that never hurried along.

Her parents' place was an unassuming two-bedroom weatherboard house in a row of similar houses. Janine parked behind her dad's Brunswick green Toyota, standing in front of a corrugated iron garage. The backyard stretched a hundred metres into an overgrown access lane at the back fence.

Behind the garage stood the relic of an old dunny, next to an aviary and a jerry-built shed. On the opposite side was a chook run, long past a rooster's crow, and a square fibro bungalow, that was to be my temporary home.

FOREVER DAY

There were garden beds and low fruit trees in between the outbuildings. You could see they had once been lovingly tended to feed a family of eight. You could picture Nelly, the milk cow, tethered to a stake in the backyard; Dad mowing the lawn neat and tidy around the front veranda while Janine and her sister were soaking up a suntan in the backyard with their cat slinking along.

This was a much-loved and lived-in family home, grown weary and old.

In a kitchen warmed by the combustion stove, I met Janine's makers.

Mum was just a much older version of Janine, the youngest of her six children. There were a lot of extra years between them, so Mum was now old and didn't move all that fast anymore. Still, she got up and gave me a heartfelt cuddle that made me feel right at home.

Dad was old and painfully skinny, a ten-pound Pom turned Australian before the war, though I don't think he ever picked up the most precious of Australian attitudes: *she'll be right, mate*. I never got a cuddle from him, and I never got to know him much better, he died within six months.

I only got to know him a little more after, when Janine told me about his illness, his war service, and how he used to keep chickens and birds, tend the vegetable patches, and take long walks with her along the bush tracks on the foreshore. Through her eyes, I remember him a lot more kindly.

My temporary home in the fibro bungalow was Janine's place. Just big enough for a bed, a desk, a cupboard, and a glory box. Janine moved into her sister's bedroom in the house. Lucy hadn't wasted time after her trip. She'd married and moved to Queensland.

Janine would sneak over in the early mornings and we'd steam up the bungalow, then she'd sneak back into the house, have a shower, and put on her face for work, teaching some innocents the ABC and the morals of life.

It finally dawned on me that I'd been invited into her cathedral, not to share her beliefs, but to accept them. I bloody well understood. We got married four weeks after.

I didn't know anybody. Gough Whitlam wouldn't have come.

The only guy I knew, and was thrilled to see, was Istvan. He arrived in a white Cadillac. Not his; borrowed from the panel beater's shop he worked for, still waiting on the final coat of paint.

Istvan was to be our driver and my personal wedding photographer. Apart from the fondue sets, the only significant luxury item I'd brought with me to Australia was a state-of-the-art 35mm reflex camera with an automatic winder and a bag full of lenses. I'd bought cars for less than that setup.

Janine, of course, had already arranged everything: the official wedding photographer, the church, the service, the children's choir from her school, the flowers, the hymns, in one of which I was leaping over the mountains like a gazelle, the wedding reception at the Tyabb Fly Inn, the bar tab, the getaway dress, and a board of checkers we played right into our wedding night.

All I had to do was get a haircut, put on a sharp suit, and show up with my brother-in-law as my best man.

FOREVER DAY

It could easily have turned out to be a day of disaster. Istvan played my Nikon like a rock star. He kept his finger on the trigger and fired off 36 frames in ten seconds flat, until the priest told him to cut it out. After the service, he drove my brother-in-law and me to the reception. Janine let someone else drive her car so it'd be ready for our getaway.

With just a bit less luck, we could've had the shortest marriage ever. Istvan drove like the devil, ready to claim his last soul. Caddies just aren't built for sharp turns. Anyway, we made it. I never let him drive any of us again.

The potentially much worse disaster could have been of Janine's making. She'd scheduled our wedding day for September 24, 1977, the day of the VFL Victorian Football final.

I had no idea then, but footy in Victoria wasn't a sport. It was a religion. Footy final day was holier than Christmas and Easter combined. You didn't drive your car, you didn't give birth, you didn't get married, and you didn't die on footy final afternoon.

It slowly dawned on me when I noticed all the men standing around with little transistor radios glued to their ears. In the men's, there was a lineup by the wash basin, not for soap and water, but to keep tabs on the score.

The footy gods smiled on us. The game ended in a draw and had to be repeated.

And just to show you that children re-live your own life, thirty years later, almost to the day, our middle daughter, Denise, celebrated her wedding on footy final day. It was in Queensland and by then, footy was played all over Australia, VFL had become AFL, and the Victorian magic was long gone.

FOREVER DAY

If I had to choose of a time, when every day was a forever day, it would have been our first years of marriage. It wasn't just us, getting to know each other. It was ignorant me, slowly blending in.

Our first home was an old farmhouse set in the middle of one hundred and twenty acres of grazing land in 203 Myers Road, Bittern. We rented it from Harley Unthank, a local apple grower. I believe it was his old family home. He had it freshly re-painted and re-carpeted. If I'd put it on a postcard, you'd know it was in Australia. A modest little two-bedroom house with a fenced garden, at the end of a long gravel driveway with a water tank, a few large gum trees and big hay shed behind. Right next to it was a piece of virgin bush, owned by the local water board. The house and the setting made it the most beautiful little Australian gem I could have wished for my start down under. You can Google Earth it. Fifty years later, it still looks virtually the same.

We were on town water, with a trickle line feeding the tank. It still required a pump that came on whenever you turned the tap on. Every so often, the pump would get clogged with debris from the tank and stop, and I had to rush out of the shower, butt naked, with shampoo all over my head, to unclog it.

Harley kept a herd of twenty or so steers for fattening on the property. Every now and then, he would come over to check on them or throw out a few bales of hay if their feed was getting low. He'd always call in for a chat. He ended every second sentence with, 'if you follow my meaning?' I thought he took me for a foreign illiterate, but he used it on Janine as well, and her English was almost as perfect as a linguist's. She was a bit scared of the steers, especially if she came home late in the dark, open the gate and drive up the long driveway in the middle of a herd of curious beasts.

Sometimes at night, we could hear gun shots from the virgin bush next door. It worried us a bit at first but over time we got used to it. It was just idiots with guns trespassing to shoot rabbits.

There were a lot of magpies nesting in the large gum trees around the hay shed. One day, a bird of prey attacked one of the nests, and two fledgling birds came tumbling down. They called for their parents in vain, so we took them in. To keep them fed with worms, I had to dig up half the backyard. They got so used to it, they thought the spade was their parent. If they were hungry, they would sit next to the spade and beg until I picked it up and dug up some more worms.

When I had to go out, Janine would put them in a cardboard box and take them to school in the boot of her car. She let the older kids feed them pet food meat during breaks. She taught the little room, prep to grade two; Dorothy Blanch took the big room, grades three to six.

We kept the magpies in the laundry most times, but every now and then we took them inside, and one or the other would sit on my shoulder and watch me type. When we thought they were mature enough, we took them outside to sleep on the lower branches of the gum tree by the gate. If there was wind or rain, we'd rush out every few minutes to check on them. They just sat there, huddled together, breaking our hearts.

One day, they just took off with the mob of the locals. For a while, they called in every now and then, but they weren't tame anymore. Even after they stopped coming, we still recognised one of them by his distinctive markings for a long time.

FOREVER DAY

I reckon an Australian magpie's song is the most beautiful sound to wake up to. All the more so with Janine next to me.

Janine also had another bird, a budgerigar called Budgie, kept in her classroom for the children to enjoy. When school was out, she'd bring Budgie home, and he became so tame that we kept him for good. He had the run of the house. We only put him in a cage when we wanted him to enjoy sunshine and a chat with the magpies. We'd hang his cage by the back door, only to find him bailed up by a butcherbird clinging to the wire, with Budgie hunkered in the furthest corner, trembling with fear. He wasn't the outdoor type of bird.

We taught him a few words. He liked to talk. He could say 'Hello' in perfect Swiss German. When I shaved, he sat on my shoulder and pecked at the shaving cream. When Janine peeled apples at the kitchen table, he hopped into the peelings and flapped his wings like he was having a bath. I never had to take him anywhere, he always found me on his own. While I typed, he'd hop onto the typewriter's carriage and ride it to the end of the line. When the little margin bell rang, he gave it a peck, and I rolled the carriage back to the other side.

I was churning out quite a bit of writing by then. Mostly run-of-the-mill stuff picked up from the local news, rebranded for the Swiss readers. I kept the TV on most of the day, letting it bubble on low. I didn't watch it much. I had a tape recorder sitting on top of the set. Whenever something caught my interest, I'd press record. I got some good money out of watching TV. The press agency had lots of small newspapers and magazines on their client list, some of my articles got picked up multiple times.

I wasn't just a cheap transcriber. If something snagged my attention, I chased it down. I'd follow up, go to locations, interview people and take pictures. We're talking pre-mobile, pre-internet, pre-anything. Landlines, hardcopies and slide film only.

When I did a piece about shark attacks, I bought in slides from Ron and Valerie Taylor, shark royalty, fifty bucks a frame. I phone-interviewed two shark experts and Janine and I took a trip to one of them; I think it was in a coastal town in South Australia. This guy had a great big tank full of sharks in a museum type setup. I thought they were mostly gummy sharks but when he used a broom to float one close to my camera, it bit him in the arm and drew quite a bit of blood. Served him right. I never liked animals being taken out of their environment and kept in captivity. Eat them or let them go, that's how I fish.

For a non-car-guy, I developed quite a liking for hot rod shows and drag racing. Janine and I went to a lot of them. I took pictures and sent them to a Swiss magazine that asked for more smoke. My press agency credentials got me right between the staging lanes and the burnout pads. Somebody lent me a pair of earmuffs, and I shot five rolls of smoke and raw power, building into a trembling heat beneath a full Christmas tree.

That fraction of a second before the green light came on must have felt like a lifetime for the two drivers, each sitting in a ten-thousand-horsepower bomb ready to blow. Then the release, five or six frames later, it was all over. The pit crews jumped for joy or shrugged their shoulders, calmly getting ready for the next run. Epic stuff. I managed to capture it all with one or two pictures out of one hundred or more. I wish I still had them.

After a year or two, I got a bit more clued up about what sold and where I could get free slides. The big companies usually were happy to supply them free of charge. I once did an article about the economical and environmental impact of mining for the Sunday supplement of a big Swiss daily. I got all the slides I needed free from BHP, even though I was quite critical of them. The eight page article paid one thousand five hundred francs, more than I got for my first book. We spent it straight away. Janine's Toyota was blowing smoke and needed new rings. We went to her car dealer who didn't wear a suit. He sold us the car he had kept in reserve for his wife: a Kingswood '72. It never let us down. Charlie with the shovel would have approved.

My debut book met the break-even point and I was invited to submit my second novel. It came out and did okay but then I got the ultimate pink slip: Sauerländer had lost too much money and the new-text-series was axed. I asked them if they had any work for me, translating young adult or children's books from English into German. Irana sent me back a postcard with no greeting and one line only: *Write your own!!* I did, but that was later.

Reading back over this chapter, I realise that it might sound like a success story. It was, for the entertainment value of it. Janine and I travelled all over the countryside in our own budget version of the Leyland brothers. We met some really weird and wonderful people, like the guy who built a house out of bottles. Like the president of the Victorian Swiss yodel club, who also happened to be the world's foremost expert on mammalian hair identification. Like Ted Pritchard, who put a steam engine into a Falcon and hissed me around the streets of Melbourne with just a whisper of an engine sound. I seem to remember that he got a substantial grant from the government to produce a prototype of his own, but the Pritchard Steamer never made it into production.

One article landed me in a snake pit, literally, in an empty swimming pool in Rosebud. I was there to interview a bloke who was about to break a South African's record of 52 days in a snake pit. He waved me down, and Janine and her older sister, Shirley, looked over the edge in utter surprise and terror.

He had a proper little camp set up. I can't remember how many snakes there were. A lot. He caught a few and held them up so I could take pictures. I nearly tripped over a couple of red-bellied black snakes trying to get him in frame. He told me not to worry, they were well fed, and it was too cold for them to move fast.

I could go on, great memories; great people, but like a lot of their stories, my own writing endeavours were not rewarded with a big monetary success. Luckily, neither Janine nor I ever worried about money or the lack of it. We enjoyed life and each other, and she was happy to keep teaching and have me pitch in what I could. But there was the question of the womb.

14

The question of the womb

I like to keep the through-line of my life in a clean arc.

Job, car, girlfriend.

Sex, drugs, and rock 'n' roll.

Marriage, making love, and children.

Death, destruction, inheritance.

I'm a simple guy. I like to see results. There were none. My Love Goddess began to wonder, too. I mean, we sparked all right, couldn't keep our hands off each other but the proof is in the puddin', right? Worry none. Janine came up with her own diabolical scheme. She told me she'd worked out when she was ovulating and when I had to be on call for duty. I kid you not. I think she cheated with some sort of counting charts, but she'd swear any oath that she not only knew when she was ovulating, but she also knew the exact right spot where she conceived.

Pretty big call for a Catholic primary school teacher.

We later marked the spots on the carpet and the kitchen table with an X. I forgot where the third X was placed. It could have been on Shoreham Beach but I might be wrong. Anyway, that's the children accounted for. I need them for proof reading so I won't embarrass them anymore.

With the first-to-be-born secured in mum's-to-be womb, I went to Centrelink to cry myself a paying job. I was still a few months short of becoming a true blue Aussie, eligible for unemployment, or any other benefits, so I was treated with the respect of old uncle scrooge: happy to give you free advice but just don't ask for money. Back then, Centrelink wasn't just sitting on the government's money bags, they also were a pretty efficient job agency. They always got me a job when I wanted one badly enough. Boy, did they come up with some pearlers!

Exhibit One: Bata Shoes, Seaford.

Bata got paid government subsidies to take on poor slobs like me to operate their shoe sole presses at minimum wage with shift work. They packaged it as a teaching course that ended with a certificate of shoe sole press operator. Janine kept mine in her glory box for a laugh. Maybe one day I'll emigrate to India and it might come in handy.

The job involved putting the uppers of a pair of shoes into a great big press that pumped out rubber or whatever and moulded and glued it as sole onto the uppers. If you made the quota, your minimum pay got slightly bumped up. Newcomers never made it. We got lumped with the odd sizes, the repairs or the one-offs that required constantly changing the moulds. I don't know how long I stayed, but I outlasted everybody in my line. The smarter ones walked out halfway through their first shift.

Exhibit Two: Armstrong Nylex Carpets

Centrelink sent me there. I don't think they had a subsidy deal. They just needed cheap process workers for their carpet line. They were a big outfit; everything had to be done by the book. I had to pass a medical and join a union. No card, no job. They put me at the end of a conveyor-belt oven, which baked glue onto carpet squares. You're right: the certificate of shoe sole presser had some relevance here. At my end of the belt, the machine covered the glued side with a plastic film. I had to keep an eye on the plastic roll, take the carpet squares out of the machine and stack them in cardboard boxes. Anybody who can read or write this sentence should not be working there. It was just the most mindless job I've ever done, barely fit for human consumption.

To make matters worse, at the front end of my line stood two of the most disgusting Australian brats I ever met. They were young, probably fresh out of grade seven. They were lazy, racist and just plain dumb. They were convinced I was German. In the mornings they'd greet me with a Nazi salute and call me a cocksucker. Innocent little me had no idea what it meant. I had to ask Janine.

Anyway, I probably could have beaten them up one at a time, but that's not me. I complained to the foreman and he made them stop. They were less rude now but they stayed dumb and lazy. Every so often they'd put a bunch of carpet squares on top of each other into the machine and have the automatic sensor switch it off. I could easily have removed the blockage, but that was not how things work in an Australian union-controlled workplace. You report the outage to the foreman. He informs the appropriate maintenance crew. They come and assess the damage. They send the electrician. He does his bit but he can't finish the job, because he needs another guy from another union to throw the mechanical switch and get us online once more.

I worked my arse off on that shitty machine. The foreman told me they needed to fill a large order of a million or whatever carpet squares. I endured it to the end. Then they sacked me. They had sold off their carpet line. Last in, first out. The foreman was really quite emotional giving me the bad news. So was I. I went home and told Janine to start packing, but my calm and steady goddess, Myers Road Bittern and hitting the Hermes soon had me back on happy days.

The foreman rang me a bit later and offered me a job on their vinyl flooring line. I had worked there quite often when the two little shits killed the carpet line. I told him to tell his company to fuck off. I told Centrelink, Process Work, Unions and Minimum Wage with Overtime to fuck off. I vowed never to work for the man again. That was the day my life began.

15

Chicken Paprikash

I went to see Istvan in Springvale at the Hungarians' place. I won't give you the address for reasons that will become obvious.

Istvan had given us a wedding present, too big to wrap up or carry: an old VW Kombi with issues. I don't think I ever told him about my first car but even if I did, how weird a wedding present to give somebody you've only met a few times.

The Hungarians' place was an old Melbourne weatherboard with a large shed shop front along a busy city street. The place was fully fenced and gated. There was no access other than the driveway. I pulled up in front of the gate and got out. There was a big yard behind the building, full of cars and car parts, spreading a long way into dense rolls of blackberries and rows of high standing tomato and sunflower plants. I sang out and eventually a man's head popped around the front door of the house.

'What do you want?'

'I'm Flicks. I'm here to see Istvan.'

'Stephen?'

'Yeah. Istvan. We met on the ship and he was at my wedding.'

'Ah, yes. The Swiss. Wait a minute, I'll get the gate for you. You can drive right into the yard.'

The guy that eventually opened the gate could have been Istvan's older brother. Maybe he was, I never asked. He didn't just open the gate. He first looked around, up and down the street; like he wanted to make sure I had no tail. When he did finally open the gate, he waved me through and pulled it shut following the rear bumper of my car. Only then did he relax. He came over to me, shook my hand and introduced himself.

'Alex. Stephen is somewhere down the bushes.'

'Alex? What's that in Hungarian?'

'The same. Alex. Have you come for your bus?'

'Which one is it?'

'The blue one down there.'

'Is it drivable?'

He was a car guy. He got the joke and grinned.

'If you put a door in it. And an engine.'

'I don't fix cars', I said. 'What would it set me back for you to do it? Do you do mechanical repairs or just panel beating?'

'We do both but I wouldn't bother. Unless you have a lot of time and know your way around cars?'

'Not my field of expertise. How much?'

'Roadworthy standard with a new paint job, ready to go, two thousand. Cash only.'

'Forget it!'

Alex laughed. 'I told you she wasn't worth it,' he said. 'Stephen said you were an accountant?'

'Was.'

FOREVER DAY

'Where do you work?'

'I'm working from home right now. I might get myself a business one of these days.'

'Accounting?'

'I don't think so. I worked in a pub for a while. People will always eat and drink.'

'Bloody right! Can you do bookkeeping?'

'I get by.'

'Could you do my books? Not for free. I'll pay you.'

'What do you need a bookkeeper for? No offence, but this place doesn't look like a business with much of a paper trail. Cash only, right?'

'No offence taken,' said Alex. 'We'll talk later. Have lunch with us in the house when you're done. Here comes Stephen.'

Istvan came out of the blackberry bushes with a big grin on his face.

'You made it,' he said. 'Seen your Kombi?'

'It's a bloody wreck, Istvan!'

'You can fix her. I'll give you a hand, if you want me to.'

'Don't bother. I need a car I can drive.'

'Okay, then. Let me show you something…'

I followed him to where he'd come from. When I navigated my way through the blackberries, I felt like I had taken a wrong turn right into one of the two houses on the road to Mount Gambier. Behind the blackberries, the sunflowers and the tomatoes, Istvan was growing weed. Rows of it.

'What do you think?'

'You're a bloody idiot, Istvan! What if they throw you out?'

'Too late. I've got my ticket.'

'You're an Australian?'

'True Blue. Want to see my citizenship certificate?'

'No! You're still an idiot. What do you do with this much weed? Sell it?'

'No. It's not just mine. Alex smokes some; Melissa puts it in her cooking.'

'Melissa?'

Alex's wife. She's Italian but she cooks a mean goulash.'

'Can you actually get high from cooking weed?'

'Maybe. Not sure. Her kids like it.'

'Holy shit, Istvan! She cooks up weed for her kids?'

'For whoever eats with us. I think she's doing Chicken Paprikash for lunch. The kids are with her ex right now, so it'll only be us. I'll ask her if you can stay.'

'Alex already invited me for lunch. He wants me to cook his books.'

'Okay then.'

FOREVER DAY

Chicken Paprikash turned out to be a creamier version of Hungarian goulash made with chicken instead of meat. Melissa was in the kitchen getting it ready. She seemed surprised that I took an interest in her cooking.

'It's just a traditional Hungarian stew,' she said. 'Alex's' mum taught me how to cook it. It's easy to make. I can give you the recipe if you want to try it yourself.'

'I'd love that. Istvan said, you cook weed with it. Surely you didn't get that from your mother-in-law?'

Melissa laughed it off with a waving motion of her hand.

'Ah, Istvan told you? Don't fall for it. It's just a prank of theirs. The boys made me put a few crushed up leaves and buds in it and pretended it made them high. It doesn't work. I've used it in a lot of my cooking, it's got a strong earthy taste to it, so I never use much. It's just a seasoning made from a plant. Greens. Good for you!'

'Are you sure?

'Of course I'm sure. I wouldn't feed it to the kids if I wasn't. Those two pot heads just pretend. Or maybe they really believe it works, like giving somebody a Panadol and pretend it's a sleeping pill. I used to do that when my mother couldn't sleep. Worked most of the time.'

'It is what you make of it.'

'What was that?'

'Just something somebody once said to me. I'm really looking forward to lunch.'

It was the best chicken dish I've ever tasted. Look up Chicken Paprikash and cook it yourself. You'd need the taste buds of a forty-smokes-a-day tragic not to fall in love with it, but you'll never get it tasting as good as Melissa's without the Hungarian secret herb.

After lunch, Alex shepherded me into what he called his office. It was just a desk and two chairs in a corner of the panel-beating shop, with overspray on every bit of the furniture.

'What do you know about panel beating?' he asked.

'It's expensive.'

He laughed like I had made a joke. It took him a while to realise that I was not laughing with him.

'Rightio! How do I account for my income without paying taxes?'

'You're a business. You don't get taxed on your income. You get taxed on the net profit.'

'No shit?'

'No shit. Look, Alex, you'll have to be a lot more specific if you want me to cook the books for you. And remember, I don't know all that much about Australian tax law.'

'Stephen said you were smart.'

'He did? He called me a bum. Several times.'

'I'll take what I can get. What do you want to know?'

'Tell me how you run your business. Somebody comes in and asks you to fix his car. What then?'

'I don't do walk-ins.'

'Who's cars are you fixing, then?'

'The Hungarians', that's who.'

'I don't even know what that means. Come on Alex, I'm your priest now, confess and I might be able to give you absolution.'

'You're a weird one. This is how it works: Zoltan comes in with a Merc that needs a new paint job. I do it and charge him two thousand cash. He picks up the Merc and hands over the cash.'

'Who is Zoltan?'

'Just a name. One of the Hungarian network.'

'Is it his car?'

'Who cares? He drives it into the yard, he pays for the job, he leaves.'

'Do you give him a receipt?'

'I'm not stupid!'

'Where do you get your paint from?'

'Zoltan.'

'Does he give you a receipt?'

'He's not stupid.'

'Do you own the property? Do you have a mortgage or do you rent?'

'All mine. Mortgage is from Zoltan.'

'But you do pay for electricity and rates. Insurance. They are not run by Zoltan. They give you a receipt.'

'Yes. Got them.'

'To summarise: You can show, what? A couple of thousand dollars in expenses and no income. You must have a lot of cash stashed away.'

'Stephen said you were smart. That's why I need you. Melissa's ex works in a government office. He hates my guts. He can make a lot of trouble for us. I don't want him to get his hands on the cash. It's for us and Melissa's kids, not for some fat cat in an office.'

'Put the money in the bank. He won't be able to touch it there.'

'I'm not stupid. Banks tell you-know-who. Not in your country, right?'

'My country is your country, Alex. I like it here. I'm not going back.'

'Just for a visit to the bank. I'll pay you for it. And if it works out, Zoltan might pay you as well.'

'Let me think about it, Alex. First I need to set up some kind of accounting system for you. Do you do your own tax returns?'

'Zoltan's friend does them. She works as a cleaner at Chadstone shopping centre. She picks up all the dockets people throw away. You need paperwork for tax returns, right?'

'She claims grocery dockets as tax deductions?'

'Not just groceries. It's a big shopping centre. There are at least two hundred other stores there.'

'And you've never been audited?'

'Why would I be? I pay taxes, like everybody else.'

'Give me your returns from the last three years. I'll see what I can do. I'll have to think about the Swiss bank account some more. It won't be cheap.'

'How much?'

'More than two thousand. Cash.'

FOREVER DAY

16

Little Red Rooster

My visit with the Hungarians had given me a lot to think about. Not just their books, but mine as well. Accounting is the same boring job the world over, but there are different degrees of it. Australia had its own blend of accounting boredom, enshrined in around two thousand pages of the *Australian Master Tax Guide*. I speed-read it over the weekend and, from then on, used it as a wedge under the faulty bedroom sash window that kept sliding shut. The tax guide was the perfect size, just thick enough to let in a sliver of air and keep the room comfortable.

Come to think of it, that's exactly what it's used for to this day, sitting on the window sill of your tax agent, letting in a sliver of hope for a tax break.

Mum's words of wisdom had come back to me over Chicken Paprikash. 'People will always eat and drink.'

I started looking for a pub to buy or rent. Trouble was, there wasn't one in sight. Here we had HMS Cerberus naval base that churned out six thousand new drunken sailors every year, and not a pub in sight. Well, not within walking distance. According to Janine, there was some long standing agreement between the council and the base, to not allow a pub within five clicks. The next drinking hole was in Hastings, five miles down the road. The Hastings pub was not for sale and even if it was, I could not have afforded it. I wasn't interested in buying anywhere else. I was just too damn happy typing stories with a bird sitting on my shoulder or go mushroom hunting or pick blackberries in our paddock on Myers Road. I didn't want to move and I didn't fancy a long commute, either.

FOREVER DAY

I scaled down my wish list to include smaller eateries, cafés or takeaways with a dining area. As it happened, something came up in Hastings that ticked a few boxes. It was a curious hybrid: part shop, part takeaway, part fishmonger, tucked inside the Permewan Wright Shopping Centre, directly opposite the Payless supermarket checkout. The centre's still there under new owners, just across from the Hastings Pub near the foreshore. Permewan Wright and Payless, however, are long gone, so I can dish on them freely.

The shop had been set up by Nick the Greek from Crib Point. After selling his own place, he kitted out mine with the cheapest, most dilapidated second-hand equipment he could scrounge, salvaged from auctions of other Nick-the-Greeks' failed ventures. He stuck his finger in the leaking bain-marie, hot-wired the failing cool room compressor, and hoped for the best. Once he'd scribbled a few pages in the takings book, he sold the business and moved on to his next tribulation-in-waiting. By now, he's probably back in Greece and owns a shipping line.

I bought the business and sold the seafood side back to Nick. He cleared out the freezers and fridges, giving me space for new tables and chairs.

After poring over the takings book, I saw that fresh fish had been the top earner, with roast chicken a close second. I added a second, four-spit rotisserie for another 24 birds, fixed the bain-marie and the cool room, gave the place a proper scrub, loaded twenty-four size twenty chickens into the rotisserie, and sold out by lunchtime. Next day I loaded up the second rotisserie and doubled my takings. Things were off to a promising start.

After a few days on the job, a man in his fifties wandered up and said, 'Hi, I'm Andy. I work here.'

FOREVER DAY

I figured he was one of the regular drunks who staggered in from the pub next door to sober up on a breast of chicken and chips. He looked the part, singlet, stubble on his chin, and a large black bandage wrapped around his right arm.

'That's news to me, Andy.'

'Didn't Nick tell you?'

'Tell me what?'

'That I work here. I peel the potatoes, cut the chips, season the chickens, load them on the trolley and wheel them into the cool room. That's my job. Love what you've done with the place.'

'Thanks, Andy. Look, I had no idea. I could really use the help. I wish Nick had told me, I couldn't find any wage records in his paperwork.'

'No paperwork. Cash only.'

'Are you Hungarian?'

'Don't be bloody stupid!'

'Come on, Andy, give me something. Where do you live?'

'Right up the road, in a shitty little one-room brick flatette. I used to work for Telecom as a linesman. Cut my arm in an accident and ended up on workers comp.'

'I don't know what workers comp means, Andy.'

'Bloody wogs know nothing!'

'I know what that means, Andy. You'd better play nice if you want your job back.'

'No offence meant. Workers compensation is a compulsory insurance that pays you pittances if you get hurt at work and can't work anymore.'

'And you still worked for Nick?'

'Do I have to spell it out? I can't do my old job, but I can peel potatoes and season chickens for a bit of cash on the side. Got it?'

'Got it. How much?'

'One hundred a week.'

'Welcome to Chickens on Hastings.'

'Is that what you call your shop? You're bloody mad, you know that?'

Andy started straight away, I mean, almost mid-sentence. He walked into the kitchen, put on an apron, and cranked up the potato peeler, another industrial relic from Nick the Greek's salvage yard. It made a hell of a racket, and it didn't just take off the spuds' jackets, it tore right into the flesh. I reckon one-third went straight down the sink.

Andy made sure the door was closed. Always. He got real mad if I opened it while he worked. He never spelt it out, but I soon got it. Workers comp.

Andy turned out to be my saviour. He wasn't shy working up front, as long as it didn't involve undue physical activity in public. Not because he was lazy. Workers comp.

It got me thinking. I asked the girls in the travel shop down from me and they put me onto their insurance broker who arranged cover for my shop as well.

Business was slowly building up. I needed more chickens. I'd inherited my supplier from Nick. His name was George, which was probably an Anglicised version of Giorgio. He was second-generation Italian, from a family that farmed broilers and roasters on the northern outskirts of Melbourne.

He called in twice or three times a week with an old panel van. He'd park in the laneway behind the shop and enter through the back door. The back of his van was filled with large slabs of ice under a tarp; the chickens were stacked on top in plastic crates. The van looked like a leaking boat in reverse. It always left a great big puddle of ice water by my back door.

It took him just minutes to load the chickens onto two trolleys and wheel them into the cool room. He'd come out, hand me his handwritten invoice, and I'd pay him with cash or cheque. He'd ask me what I needed for the next run, and take off. It all went like clockwork. I never got to talk to him much.

I was still way over my head with work. I needed more help, and it walked right in. Sue, one of the young girls who worked at the bakers' next door had lost her job. Fresh oven-baked bread wasn't selling all that well back then, when the choice was mainly between loaf and sliced.

She simply walked over, still in her short-skirt work outfit from the bakery, and started serving coffee right away. Andy was over the moon. He'd sit there and watch her bend over to check what colour underwear she wore. He told me he loved big bottoms in women.

I told him to zip it. I didn't have room for a horny old rooster in Chickens on Hastings.

FOREVER DAY

My two years were by now well and truly up. I felt Australian, the '80s were just around the corner, so was our first child; time for me to become an Australian citizen. The ceremony was held in the Hastings Council offices, with Peter Ainsworth presiding.

I knew Peter through Janine. His family lived in Crib Point, and Janine was friends with Geraldine, one of nine children. Janine spent a lot of time with the family. They were an amazing lot, quirky and eccentric to the max, close to standing-on-a-table-naked-and-singing-to-the-full-moon crazy, but intelligent and brilliant all the same. If there ever was a book worth writing, it should be about the Ainsworth family of Crib Point.

Anyway, Peter was a character. RSL member, councillor, and champion town crier. I met him at one of the family's dos and a couple of times when I dropped in at Andy's place. Peter was a diabetic and not allowed to drink, so he'd sneak in a couple at Andy's on the way home.

There was only me to be turned blue in the council chambers. I don't think Peter had conducted any of these ceremonies before. He was a lot more nervous than I was.

The pledge of allegiance back then went: "I, insert, insert, renouncing all other allegiance, do swear that I will be faithful and bear true allegiance to Her Majesty Queen Elizabeth the Second, Her Heirs and Successors according to law."

Peter read part of the pledge, and I had to repeat it. He stumbled a bit over the words, and when he came to the last bit, he said: "Queen Elizabeth, her hairs and successors…" We all cracked up, and he tried again, but by now it was all a big hoot.

FOREVER DAY

You know, he might've done it on purpose. I wouldn't put it past him.

So there you have it. Not only was I an Aussie, I was also a brand-new subject of Queen Elizabeth and her hairs. The bit about renouncing all other allegiance was technically treason. You can only renounce your Swiss citizenship under certain, hard to meet, circumstances, and it's not by saying it or turning around three times and saying it.

As soon as your foot touches down on Swiss soil, you're back on their tax radar, the electoral roll, and the army will hand you a brand-new assault rifle and 24 rounds in a sealed tin can to store in your attic and bring to your next inspection or the mandatory refresher course.

Only death can set you free.

The Australians didn't give me a gun, but I got a Bible from the Queen, a citizenship certificate from the Australian Government, and a potted gum tree from the Hastings Shire, and all it cost me was beer for everybody in the pub.

Thank you, Australia. You got two for the price of one.

Soon after, back at the ranch, Janine was ready to pop. After a mad rush to hospital and a few pushes in vain, she was temporarily put out of her misery with a caesarean, and I got to see our baby girl first.

I went home to my Australian mum and used her phone to ring my parents with the good news. I felt the arc of my life had finally touched ground, exactly where I was meant to be.

17

Eleven herbs and one spice

Back in the chicken shop, Andy was getting antsy about his upcoming medical. I never questioned him about his injury; I just assumed it was real.

To stay on workers comp, he had to see one of the Telecom-assigned practitioners in the better end of Melbourne, where Beka was selling cupcakes to rich Australians she hoped to date.

I seem to recall it happened twice a year, so every six months he must've felt like his life was on the chopping block once more. There are two sides to every story. You can take Telecom's side, I'll stick with Andy.

Andy took half a day off to see one of his mates. He came back with a wet hessian bag, and I knew straight away what was in it: crays.

He put it in the cool room and we sat down for a talk.

'Crayfish, Andy? What's up?'

'The thing is, I told, insert, insert, Dr Whatever-His-Name-Was that I go out potting for crays with my mate. He reckons that's okay for the condition I'm in. So every time I go to see him, I bring him a few crays. As kind of proof. Costs me a bloody fortune, but I'm on the hook now.'

'I hope it works out for you, Andy.'

It did. He was back, happy as Larry and horny as ever, trying to find out what colour pants Sue wore on the day.

FOREVER DAY

Andy had a Telecom mate, Steve, who called in every day for coffee and snacks. Steve was about the same age as Andy but skinnier and better kept. He always dressed immaculately with a jacket and tie. He had a marked limp and walked with the help of a stick. He too, was on workers comp. Now with Andy, you could flip a card and it could fall either way. Steve's card would always land showing its face. He was clearly broken. I mean, you could see that his leg was kind of twisted, with the foot pointing to the left. You have to be rubber man to fake that.

When Andy wasn't peeling spuds or seasoning chickens behind the closed door, he'd sit with Steve and they'd swap Telecom war stories that always ended up right where they sat: on workers comp. Apart from closing the door and worrying about his next crayfish delivery, Andy was a lot more relaxed about it. Steve, on the other hand, was a worrier to the point of being paranoid.

If I had a bit of time to spare, I'd bring him his coffee and sit with him. One day, he sat down at a different table, right next to the main aisle between us and the Payless, looking towards the main entry.

'Dick's following me,' he said.

'What dick?'

'Telecom dick. Parked in front of my house and jacked up his car to change a tyre. I watched him from the front veranda. When I caught his eye, he motioned me to come over, so I walked right up to him.

"Can you give me a hand?" he said.

I just pointed at my leg and walked away.

"Thanks a lot!" he shouted after me. He must've thought I was stupid. It's the oldest trick in the book.'

'What if he really had a flat and just wanted you to hold the wheel nuts or the wrench?'

'I won't risk it. Dicks are everywhere. They must be on a schedule. Show up three or four times a year, never the same guys, sitting in a car opposite or walking along the street with a camera, pretending to take pictures of seagulls.'

'All this effort for one man. Were you on a high salary?' I asked.

Steve laughed so loud I could see it hurt him.

'After I came out of hospital, they kept me on and put me in an office on apprentice's wages. Retraining, see? Timesheets, expense dockets, bookkeeping stuff. I tried, but I just couldn't hack it. I can't sit and I can't stand; I can't move and I can't stay still. I'm just floating on minimum comp minus pay-as-you-go tax with a Telecom dick breathing down my neck.'

Tough. You're married, right? Does your wife work?'

'She has to. Not much around. Marg's got no qualifications other than being a good wife. She takes on some real shitty jobs to make ends meet.'

'Do you think she'd like to work for me?'

'I'm sure she'd love to. She likes what you've done to the joint. I couldn't stand the stink of fish. Much nicer now, and you seem to be doing okay. What job do you have in mind?'

'Everything. Working behind the counter. Cooking, serving, the lot. It would be full-time.'

'Even better! But it has to be by the books. No Andy deal. Paycheque and all.'

'All by the books, payslip, insurance, and group certificate.'

'I'll tell her. She'll probably come running all the way over straight away.'

'Good. What about you?'

'You know that I can't work.'

'You can keep books, right?'

'Even if you pay me cash, I don't want to risk it. You shouldn't either. You could land in a lot of hot water.'

'I won't pay you. I'll pay Marg. She'll just be on a better wage.'

Steve looked at me with a sly grin.

'Do they teach you that in Swiss accounting schools?'

'You have to know the rules to bend them.'

'Okay. You've got yourself a bookkeeper. I only work from home. Call it vocational rehabilitation.'

Should I have felt guilty? Get real! Here was the biggest Australian company in 1980, twice the size of BHP, making huge money with a state owned monopoly, hounding a poor bastard who'd given them a limb. I would've gladly taken on a few more of their victims, but all my vacancies were now filled.

FOREVER DAY

Marge turned out to be a gem. She blossomed in the shop and ran it far better than I did. I got to spend more time writing, with baby girl trying hard to join Budgie on top of the typewriter. She just managed to hold onto the desk and pull herself up on wobbly legs. Life had slowed down and turned domestic, and it felt right.

Until the landlord hit me with the big hammer. At the time I opened Chickens on Hastings, the landlord was going through a major restructuring process, selling off or reorganising its assets. If you ever hear "restructuring" or "reorganising", run for the hills. Somebody always has to pay, and it's everybody from the owners down.

They increased my rent by one hundred per cent. Not the best way to make friends with your tenants. We met in the court of arbitration and I got a partial reprieve, but still ended up paying way too much in base rent. On top of that, my outgoings all of a sudden hit boiling point. I won't bore you with details, but the long and the short of it is: you've got a great big building with lots of little shops and one big shop. The big shop brings in the customers, so it pays nothing for air-conditioning, rates, and upkeep of the entire building. All the little shops, like mine, the baker, the butcher, the travel agent and so on, were the ones lumped with keeping the Payless customers comfortable. It sucks, but it's what it is, if it's in the lease. Fighting that one would've taken too much effort with little chance of success.

Bark it, fix it, or vanish. I had done all the barking, and I wasn't going to walk. I had to crank up business. By now, I'd hit about the limit of roast chickens I could sell in a day. I needed a new snare to lure in more customers.

I had never paid much attention to the way Andy seasoned the birds. We had inherited it from Nick the Greek. The seasoning came ready-mixed in a great big sack. Andy would put a few handfuls into a bowl, add salt and a bit of water, and smear the paste all over the chickens before letting them settle in the cool room overnight. The seasoning had lots of different herbs in it and made the roasted chickens look and taste good. Like everything else we needed in the shop, the bag of seasoning came in a van pulling up at the back door.

You have to understand that in those days, Kentucky Fried Chicken outlets were the hottest thing in takeaway. In Australia, they had twice or three times as many stores as McDonald's. Colonel Sanders had come up with his eleven-secret-herbs-and-spices recipe a long time ago and, if legend is true, offered it for sale over a thousand times. He did sell it to restaurants and other chicken shops until the KFC franchise bought him out for two million dollars plus extra for his mug shot for life.

I read somewhere that the Colonel made his first million at sixty-five. Unlike the Colonel, I had youth and a lot more time to catch up. But more importantly, I had something he never had: the fuse that lights the fire. Chicken Paprikash, the Hungarian way. Eleven herbs and one spice. Sue me, KFC. This one is all mine.

I took a trip to the Hungarians with good news: I was going to be their accountant. Well, Steve was. But that was between him and me.

'What about the other thing?' asked Alex.

'One thing at a time. I had a look at your old tax returns. I'm surprise you haven't been audited. You have virtually no receipts and tons of deductions. You're losing money year over year. Eventually somebody is going to ask you lot of questions. We'll have to fix it.'

'How?'

'You'll have to start showing income. Give Zoltan invoices for the cars you paint and make him give you invoices for the paint and whatever else he sells to you. You can pay cash but you have to sign for it.'

'What's the point? It still ends up as nothing.'

'If it's nothing, it has to be a traceable nothing. Auditable. Do you understand?'

'Okay. I'll give you papers. You're not going to charge me two thousand dollars for that bit of useless advice, are you?'

'It might save your arse, but no. We'll swap. I need a big bag full of the stuff Melissa puts in her Chicken Paprikash.'

'You want weed?'

'Greens, but not as bloody big leaves. I want them crushed the Melissa way. You write me an invoice for seasoning; I write you an invoice for bookkeeping advice. We have two valid transactions and yet, no money changes hands.'

'You make a lot of work over nothing,' said Alex. 'It will take a while. Stephen can bring it down when it's ready. So what about the other thing?'

'How much are we talking about?'

'I asked Zoltan. He's in. We want you to do a test run with one hundred thousand. '

'Wow! You trust me with that much?'

'Zoltan had you checked out. He knows where you live.'

'You're not threatening me, are you Alex?'

'Just a look-see. Make sure you are a responsible family man. It's a lot of money.'

I didn't like the way he said it. I liked even less that he was right.

'I don't like the way you put it, Alex. I'll have to think about it some more. If either of you ever mentions my family again, we're done.'

18

A suitcase full of money and a cricket bat

I was itching to put Melissa's recipe to the test, but before the bag of Alex's goodies arrived, I had a phone call from Dad. I knew it was bad news, because Dad never rang. Calling his children was Mum's job. Dad wasn't a phone guy. To breach the distance, he yelled: 'You have to come home, right away! My, Swiss insert, Swiss insert, sisters are suing me!'

'Take a breath, Dad! I can hear you. No need to shout. What's it all about?'

'You know, the deal you stitched up with the state government? They're suing me for their share of Dad's estate.'

'The pub? I didn't stitch up a deal. They bulldozed right over us.'

'Well, you made them pay a lot of money. Now my two greedy little sisters are suing for their share.'

I hadn't made them pay a lot of money; the government-appointed valuers had, but why hurt Dad's paternal pride?

'Just calm down, Dad. We'll sort it all out. Where do we stand right now?'

'Their lawyer lodged a claim with the court. I've got the statement of claim right here in front of me. All one hundred pages of it.'

'Sounds like a linguist. Who is their lawyer? Do you know him?'

'Don't know him. Some interstate guy, wait a minute, here it is: Wongamong, Notary and Solicitor in Lucerne.'

'When did you receive the claim?'

'Don't know for sure. A couple of weeks ago. I had to let off steam first and we're kind of busy with the new pub.'

'We've only got thirty days to lodge a defence, right?'

'Where does it say that?'

'Don't worry about it. I'll fax a motion for extension of time to the court. They'll grant it, given our circumstances. I can't just hop on a plane. I'll have to organise my own stuff first.'

'Do that! And bring the family. I'll pay the fare if you need help.'

'I'll be fine. I'll have to talk to Janine first. How's the new pub going?'

'Like a rocket. I wish you were still here, running the window. The waitresses always loved you. You were that quick.'

'I've made my choice, Dad. I found my home. I need a lot more space than Switzerland.'

'We know and we're happy for you. We can still be sad, though, right?'

'Same, same.'

Before I pick up a suitcase full of money from Alex, I'll have to jump back a number of years to my second year at the Notary Publics. In Switzerland, every real estate sale went through a Notary Publics' office. The notary wrote the contract, made sure the parties were paid, taxes were collected, and all the relevant authorities were informed. There were no real estate agents in sharp suits or high heels in Switzerland, and our fee was a pittance. Our wages were paid by the government.

It might come as a surprise to today's card- and phone-wielding cash paupers that quite a number of real estate transactions were settled in cash, over the counter. I don't make this up. You'd have somebody buy an old house for three hundred thousand francs, hand it over in three hundred crisp one-thousand-franc notes, and my boss would pass them on to eighteen-year-old me, to walk the cash to the bank about two miles down the road.

'What about security?' you ask. Here is how my boss handled it: he made me stuff the cash into my trouser and jacket pockets, carry a small leather briefcase stuffed full of newspaper, and not to put up a fight if someone went for the briefcase.

So now you might understand why picking up one hundred thousand dollars from the Hungarians wasn't a big deal. The volume did surprise me, though; it was all in twenties and fifties, neatly bundled with rubber bands. I stacked them in a long carry-on, together with a cricket set for Herbert, a former work colleague who was planning a trip down under. In winter he played ice hockey in an amateur club. Still tough enough to do a lot of damage to his body, which needed mending over the summer break. I thought if I got him onto cricket, he might have a better winter.

Qantas didn't fly into Zurich. We had to fly to Frankfurt and take a Lufthansa flight from there. Baby girl was two and a half by now, fast enough to escape if left unattended. So was the luggage. I didn't let it out of my sight. We had to wait three hours for our connecting flight. I saw a sign for a bathroom. If you think that means a toilet, you're from somewhere else. Janine and baby girl were thrilled. It was a decent-sized room with a bathtub big enough for all three of us to fit. We rented it for two hours and never boarded a plane cleaner or more refreshed.

Our plane to Zurich was a DC-9. We sat close to the curtain between first and second class. Shortly after take-off, we could hear a loud alarm bell ringing in the cockpit. It went for a few seconds and stopped. So did the plane. I don't mean we crashed, we just stopped climbing. Looking out the window, it felt like we were suspended in mid-air. After a while we levelled out and turned. None of that felt right. Janine and I were holding hands and whispered words of assurance and eternal love.

We had almost completed a full turn when the captain's voice came over the intercom.

'This is your captain speaking. I'm so sorry I messed up and over-revved one of the engines so badly that I had to shut it off. We'll return to the airport to have a look-see. There is absolutely no problem flying and landing this plane on one engine only, unless I mess up again. Please don't hate me.'

Of course, he didn't say it like that. Pilots are voice-trained in that reassuring, deep and rich, sonorous tone that reduces everything to a minor technical issue, except if you can actually see flames in the fuselage or a wing coming off.

We weren't very high up. Close enough to the ground to see the airport's rescue trucks speeding to the runway. I guess I should have felt reassured, but I was not.

Kudos to the pilot and crew. Perfect touchdown on the runway centreline, smooth taxiing and an orderly debarkation saw all passengers huddled together in a designated holding area. We were given a voucher for drinks and snacks and a choice of boarding a different flight leaving in four hours or waiting for our plane to be fixed, with an estimated departure time of two hours.

We had a quick family conference. Janine and I favoured waiting. We'd been in the air or in transit for over thirty hours by now. What's more, as Janine pointed out, 'I'd rather fly with a fixed mistake than a fresh one.'

Baby girl didn't have an opinion. She was fast asleep.

Flying into Zurich Kloten Airport always reminds me how small and beautiful Switzerland is. As the plane glides down over perfectly geometric fields, deep greens and bright yellows, you feel as though you're approaching an architect-designed model farm on the edge of a picture-perfect city. Behind it, the Limmat River and sparkling blue Lake Zurich stretch toward the snow-topped Alps.

Homecoming. You can't deny it.

'How absolutely beautiful,' said Janine. 'Why don't we live here for a while?'

'It looks different on a rainy day,' I said, 'or under a blanket of high stratus through most of winter.'

'Don't pretend you're over it, Flicks. I saw tears in your eyes.'

'Do you really mean it? Living here?'

'I wouldn't mind. If we can afford it.'

She looked me straight in the eyes. She wasn't asking. She just let it hang there.

FOREVER DAY

'Okay,' I said. 'When we can afford it.'

Immigration checked my brand-new Australian passport.

'The third one today,' he said.

'Third of what?'

'Third Swiss travelling with an Australian passport.'

He didn't stamp it, just handed it back. He wasn't unfriendly, but I wondered what he really meant. The third turncoat?

From Immigration, you walked straight into Customs. I'd passed through a few times before. Security back then was minimal. They weren't looking for bombs, just excess duty-free alcohol and cigarettes. Taxes are sacrosanct in Switzerland.

The customs officer asked me to open my carry-on, lined with bundles of red and yellow. He didn't say a word. He picked up the cricket bat and examined it.

'Never seen one like this before. What is it?'

I told him.

He took out the stumps and bails, weighed the ball in his hand.

'That would hurt,' he said, putting everything back.

'Won the lottery?' he asked.

'Thinking of settling down. Maybe buying a house.'

'Good luck with that,' he said.

FOREVER DAY

See, that's one thing I like about the Swiss. Too polite to ask about money. They just have it.

Dad and Lisa were waiting by the exit. Lisa had her daughter Nadine with her, we'd never met before. She was just a bit older than our girl, Corinne. We all hugged and compared children, while Dad grew impatient to move on. Parking fees were killers.

Dad drove us home to the Honegger house and impatiently waiting Mum. She'd visited us a year earlier, so she was the only one who knew Corinne.

I'd only seen pictures of the new pub. It was a one-storey building with a few outside tables and colourful sun umbrellas out front, and a large parking lot at the back. Inside were a bar and a dining area, big enough to seat one hundred and ten. The kitchen gleamed with stainless steel, a far cry from anything I'd ever worked in. Downstairs was a big wine cellar and a cool room behind glass walls, holding the beer kegs, hooked up to the CO_2 bottles that drove the beer to the taps above. It looked a lot like an operating theatre in a hospital.

Mum was itching to show us my old room on the first floor. It was still there, but surprise! Mum and Dad had installed a kitchen and a new toilet right next to it. There was already a large, old-fashioned bathroom up there, with a claw bath big enough to bathe a horse, and two extra bedrooms nobody used.

'All for you. If you ever need it,' said Mum.

Janine and I looked at each other and smiled.

'Thanks, Mutti,' said Janine.

FOREVER DAY

Four of my old friends were waiting for us in the pub. We sat down with them at the corner table, on two wooden benches Dad had rescued from the old pub. Jetlag snuck up on us like fog in twilight, making us wonder what time of day we were up to. Corinne got cranky and needed sleep. Janine left with her gladly, to find a bed. I battled on, trying to catch up with my friends. I heard us talking about the old days like they'd happened a lifetime ago.

I used to cook with them on weekends. Nothing fancy, just stuff we could throw into a dented old pot. Italian-style soups with rock hard salami cut into thick chunks, smothered in tomato, onion, garlic and herbs, left to simmer for two hours until the donkey in the salami was as tender as velveted beef.

In summer, we'd catch trout in the creek, wrap it tightly in foil and cook it in the hot ashes of a large fire with spuds. You could never match our meals in any of the best restaurants. Not because ours were better, but because it was us. In our time.

It came to me right there and then. You can't live two lives at once. You leave one and hanker for the other. You go back and think about where you came from. You could spin around forever and never touch ground.

I think they were disappointed when I left.

The next day I woke up happy as Larry. The last thought I'd taken into sleep had settled into a simple truth: you can't live two lives at once, but you can live in two places.

Swiss chocolate box holiday time. Especially for Corinne.

Dad used to buy in bulk at Cash and Carry's wholesale store. In the living room, he had an old-fashioned bar-type wall unit with a mirrored bar. He kept it stocked with chocolate bars. No matter when we visited, it was always full. Over time, all three of our children headed straight for the bar when we arrived. Janine tried to put her foot down, but it made no difference. I reckon Corinne gained two pounds before we left.

I took my carry-on to the bank I had dealt with in the fireplace days. The manager was happy to see me; he knew vaguely who I was. He had one of the clerks take the bag with the money to be counted in a back room, while we set up a Form-B account, custom tailored as an auto-renewable term deposit with fixed interest. All I was required to supply was the assurance, that I knew the account holder. No name, just a twelve-digit number. Completely legal and above board.

Them were the days of Swiss banking.

With the Hungarians' business taken care of, it was time to address Dad's.

I arranged a meeting with my aunties' solicitor in Lucerne. I dropped Janine and Corinne at the Swiss Museum of Transport, the school excursion emergency-go-to when bad weather wrecked a hike. In our family, it was known as the press-the-buttons place.

I found the solicitor's office in the old part of town. He was cordial. Twice my age and three times as experienced, I knew it wouldn't be plain sailing. He, of all people, understood what happens to families when you put a pot of money on the dinner table instead of a fondue.

I asked what figure might settle the dispute.

He smiled. 'A third for each client' he said, 'plus costs.'

He'd made a living out of family fondues eaten with knives. We shook hands as we parted.

'See you in court,' he said, without malice.

'Give my best to my aunties.' I replied.

I would have loved to settle without court, for Dad's sake. He wasn't taking it well. Still, one third each would have been the worst possible outcome in a court loss. Anything better was kind of a win. I was confident that I could settle for better.

I made Dad see a doctor, for probably the first time in thirty years. His readings were sky-high on everything you shouldn't be high on. Straight off a cardiac surgeon's favourite-clients list. I got the report just in time for the court case.

Dad was extremely nervous. It made him feel unwell. I would've left him out of it, but the court insisted all parties be present. On the way there, I asked him once more what his hurt-figure for a settlement was. Up until then, he'd insisted on naught.

'You fix it for me, Flicks.'

I tabled Dad's medical and he went home. Arguments were already laid out in the claim and the response. The sisters insisted Dad had made a lot of money on the pub he'd bought cheap from his own father. Our argument was that he'd been forced to sell, and had used all the profits to build a new pub.

The court was to decide and force a settlement. We settled for fifty thousand each, plus shared costs. Way less than a third and it wasn't because of me. Every member of that court had grown up in the village, with our family pub right in the heart of it. They went so far as to list some of the memorable pub events they fondly recalled. They didn't settle for us. They settled for the village and the pub.

Money matters dealt with, it was our time to enjoy the rest of the holiday. It's funny how something familiar can look different through the eye of an outsider. Riding the train to work isn't the same as riding it for a meal in the city. Visiting a restaurant in Zurich's old town with your wife isn't the same as inhaling a sandwich between lectures.

Janine had asked for a romantic dinner, and I took her to a place I knew. We ate chateaubriand with asparagus and drank a St Emilion wine half our age. When the flower girl arrived with her basket of red roses, Janine waved her over and gave her a tenner for a single stem. She handed it to me.

'Here's to the pitter-patter of new feet.'

She wasn't sure yet, but given her mythical command over ovarian tracking and conception, I had no doubt we were on the road for more. Enter baby girl number two, Denise.

19

Branching out

My Telecom crew had the chicken place humming, steady as she goes.

I rang Alex and told him the deal was done.

'I'm sure your family's happy to have you back,' he said. I wasn't sure how to take it. Maybe he was smarter than I'd given him credit for.

'Your bag of greens is ready for collection,' said Alex. 'Come by train. Stephen has a company car waiting.'

I was sure I heard someone laugh out loud in the background. When I arrived at the panel shop, I found out why. Istvan had sold our wedding-present Kombi and replaced it with a VW Beetle, freshly coated in burgundy red.

Alex took me into his two-chair office. I handed over the bank details and a stack of transfer request forms, then explained how to use them.

'Just fax one of these to the bank and they'll send the money wherever you want.'

'Zoltan will need to see that it works,' he said.

'Great. This is the invoice for my work. Bank details are on it. Pay me through the account, I'll send confirmation when it lands.'

'Four thousand two hundred and fifty dollars? You said you'd do it for the airfare.'

FOREVER DAY

'I took the family. You know why, right?'

He didn't flinch.

With my bag of dried and crushed cannabis from Alex's panel shop plot, I set about testing the waters. Alex's lot smelled grassy, with an earthy taste from the leaves, but the buds added a surprisingly strong nutty and peppery flavour. I was sure that's exactly what Melissa had used in her Paprikash mix.

A quick note to the potheads puffing half-dried weed cured in the pissing-down rain of Scotland, smelling like wet peat and rotten eggs: this wasn't remotely like that.

I got Andy to whip up a small bowl of his usual seasoning. Then I made a few test batches until I found the right mix: one spoonful of Melissa's mix to ten of Andy's. To match Melissa's Chicken Paprikash recipe, I added four spoonfuls of sweet paprika and one of garlic powder. Roast Chicken Paprikash was born.

For the record: 10:1:4:1

We stacked one rotisserie with our usual chicken mix, the other with our new and improved Roast Chicken Paprikash.

On day one, I ran a quick blind test up and down the aisle. The two young hairdressers went for Paprikash. The travel agent called it a draw. The butcher hated both, because I didn't buy my chickens from him. The real estate agent was out on a job, but his secretary preferred Paprikash. The bottle shop staff was too busy to eat right then, but they came back later and said they liked both. The baker and his wife were split.

Do the math.

FOREVER DAY

The paying customers were slower to warm to it. But eventually, Roast Chicken Paprikash edged ahead of our traditional mix. I had a stack of flyers printed and dropped them off at the shops around town. It brought in more customers. Eventually, we dipped the old recipe and stuck with Chicken Paprikash, seasoned with eleven herbs and one spice.

After three months, our sales were up thirty percent.

As Melissa had predicted, nobody ever commented on the cannabis part of the seasoning. Clearly, it had no noticeable effect. I had fallen for the placebo effect once more.

Back in '72 at the ice rink in Wetzikon, just near enough for me to walk. Everyone I knew was there for The Who. And believe it or not, André Béchir, the guy who brought them to Wetzikon, was the only person who ever signed our band. He was from the same town, not much older than us. I saw him at the concert and we said hello. I think he remembered the bad review we got. We all have to start somewhere.

There was a big crowd waiting to get in. A lot of pushing and shoving. It didn't help that André's lot had hired the Hells Angels as security. I don't think they had the right temperament for ushers. I believe they weren't re-hired after the bad press they attracted in Wetzikon.

Eventually, we all sat down on the concrete floor poured over the refrigeration pipes. There was a long delay, Pete Townshend was still in transit from Munich. While we waited, a few joints and bongs started making the rounds. Then more. Until there was a thick, sweet cloud drifting over the ice rink.

And here's the thing: none of us smoked anything other than tobacco. Scout's honour. But when the concert was over and we regrouped outside, most of us felt stoned. Of course there was some passive smoking, but not enough to explain it. Never. And yet, I felt it. So did most of the others.

In the right crowd it might have worked. Problem was, the right crowd wasn't my crowd anymore. I didn't do drugs, I didn't smoke weed or hash and I frankly, other than Istvan and Alex, I didn't know anybody who did. They were yesterdays' crowd. Worlds apart now from a husband and a dad, private health insurance and progressive dinners with other parents in town.

It was on one of these dinners that one of Janine's friends commented on the roast chickens from my shop.

'You should sell the recipe,' she said. 'I'd buy it in a flash.'

I wasn't going to give up my secret, but I was happy to make up a few baggies. Well, Janine was. She was good at making nice things out of nothing. Teacher training with the nuns, years of showing little school how to draw a face that didn't look like a sun, filling the arts cupboard with her own money until Gough Whitlam sent her a cheque for one hundred dollars. Only Australian Prime Minister ever to give a damn about education. She would've married him if she hadn't run into me.

I had a label printed: a roast chook on a bed of green okra leaves, looking the part. Cannabis was still illegal, and I didn't fancy spending time in a room with a small window and bars. The blurb read: *"Our seasoning is a sacred blend: eleven herbs and spices for flavour, plus one secret leaf for kicks."*

We sold out in a month. Janine kept making new baggies, very arty, with ribbons and all, heavily pregnant with Denise, who was no doubt infused with Mum's art. One caesarean later, we were a family of four.

FOREVER DAY

We went out and bought new furniture, just because we could afford it. In hindsight, it was a mistake. Everything we had in our first home was made by us, for us and could never be replaced.

Janine dug out our lounge suite from under her sister's house. She sanded it, repainted it, and reupholstered it in her happy colour, yellow. Harley had left one cupboard behind, and we had Janine's furniture from the bungalow, all restored by her. I bought my monster of a fake art nouveau desk from Ledbetter's junk shop in Crib Point, along with a sideboard painted kitchen-white, its leadlight glass doors broken. It took me two weeks to strip the paint and fix the lead and the glass.

My office chair was an old deck chair with a hard-stuffed cushion as a backrest. Janine built shelves out of painted and paper-lined apple crates, and she re-laminated a fifties kitchen table and four chairs. Our drinking glasses came from Vegemite jars, our cups were second-hand but clean. Janine never accepted stains or chips.

Our fridge had no handle, which caused our first fight. Goddess didn't know that I can fix anything, except cars. When Janine invited some snooty schoolteachers from Hastings over for drinks, they pitied us, and it made us proud.

We should've kept the lot.

I hit the road in the Hungarian's company car, an esky full of cold chicken bits and a basket of seasoning bags on the back seat. I targeted takeaways and cafés around the Mornington Peninsula and Western Port Bay. Dozens of tourist destinations lined the way, some were happy to give my seasoning a try.

I was the Aussie Colonel Sanders on a quest, ventured further afield, all around Port Phillip Bay and into the city, collecting more EOIs, expressions of interest, as the Australian Government so beautifully calls them, while trying to lure skilled workers from countries that probably can't afford to lose them.

My EOIs were quite successful. After two months on the road, the orders started coming in, just in time to offset an unexpected drop in roast chicken sales.

Coles must have a secret sniffer device that tells them where chickens are sold in numbers. They built a new supermarket just down the road and roasted their own. I felt it. Payless felt it too. So did all the other shops in our by-now somewhat dated centre.

One down, one up. I got over it. I was still ahead and my prospects suddenly brightened.

One early Monday morning, George with the chicken van called in with his routine delivery. When he handed me the docket, I noticed that he was kicking his heels. He had something to get off his chest. I waited for him the get it out.

'Papa wants to talk to you,' he said.

'Your dad wants to talk to me? Why?'

'No my dad. Papa. Lunch Friday at our place. I'll bring Friday's delivery and take you there and back after.'

'What's it all about? My chicken orders?'

'Don't ask me. Ask Papa.'

It was quite a long drive through the city and into the rural holdings in the north. I hadn't realised how far my chickens had to travel to get paprikashed.

FOREVER DAY

It wasn't a comfortable ride by any measure. George wasn't much of a talker, and the chicken funeral van smelled awful once the melted ice water loosened the crust left behind from the last chicken's final journey. I tried to make conversation, hoping to find out where we were headed, but all he said was that chickens ran in his family.

After two and a half hours, we finally pulled up. Not at a farm, but in front of a large, imposing house, bricks and balustrades, Roman arches and long columns, all topped with a terracotta tiled roof.

'This is your place?' I asked, surprised.

'Papa's place. Follow me.'

There wasn't a chicken in sight. Just manicured lawns, lush paddocks with white fences, and rustic wooden stables with open doors revealing white horses and shiny black cars.

I followed George through the front door, across the hall, and straight out the back, onto a wide patio that ran the full length of the building. A low sandstone wall enclosed the space, topped with boxes of red and pink geraniums that framed the view over the paddocks and stables. An old grape vine twisted around one of the columns, its thick trunk spiralling upward, shoots gripping the rafters to form a leafy canopy.

A long, chunky table filled half the patio, surrounded by enough chairs to seat a wedding or a wake.

George headed for an older man at the head of the table. He wasn't as imposing as my mind had made Papa out to be, short, with a neatly trimmed grey beard and a brown herringbone flat cap pulled low.

FOREVER DAY

'Papa, this is Felice, the Swiss,' said George.

Papa stretched out one arm to shake my hand.

'We finally meet,' he said. 'You're younger than I thought.'

'I'm sorry to disappoint you, Sir.'

'Don't be so bloody formal, man! You're not at high school. Call me Papa.'

'Like the Pope?'

He grinned.

'Just like il Papa. Are you a good Catholic, Felice?'

'I married one, and the children are. Sometimes I pretend to be Catholic, when the Jehovah's Witnesses walk up the driveway and Janine shoves me out the door to stop them coming in. She still wants me to give them twenty cents for a copy of the Watch Tower. She's got a good heart. Doesn't like to see them walk all the way back with nothing to show for their efforts.'

'I like a good family man,' said Papa. 'Stable. Lots to give…and to lose.'

Right then, I knew this was going to be a wedding party.

'Move one up, Lorenzo,' said Papa to the man beside him. 'Let Felice sit by my side.'

Everyone to his right shifted one seat up in a silent game of musical chairs.

'Bring a glass for our friend,' he said to nobody in particular. 'Red or white?'

FOREVER DAY

'Red.'

'And bring a plate.'

I've met people like that in the pub, usually overweight old men in tight jackets, flopping into a chair and barking out their order like the whole bar was taking notes. In our pub, that was a sure way to get really bad service.

Not here. Out of nowhere, a glass and a plate of cold meat and salad appeared like magic.

'Salute,' said Papa as we clinked glasses. 'Dig in, Felice, while I tell you a story.'

There was a lot of digging to be done. My antipasto platter was piled high with salami, prosciutto, mozzarella, olives, and artichoke hearts, with chunks of bread, tomatoes, nuts, grapes, and colourful spreads I didn't recognise. Salad was on the side.

'I have this friend of a family friend,' said Papa. 'He tells me a story about a man whose wife left him for another, with three precious little children in between. Sad, isn't it? You'd feel for a man like that, having children of your own.'

'So this man goes to court, and they allow him to see his children for one day, while his ex-wife can smother them with her love the rest of the week. Now this man cares deeply for their wellbeing. He wants to make sure they'll have everything they need for a good start. Money, mostly, if you follow my meaning.'

'Now this man comes crying to my friend of the family and says a Swiss has helped that other man take the money off the children. And asks me to do something about it. What would you do if you were me? Send somebody around?'

FOREVER DAY

'You're talking about Melissa? What's wrong with you! You must have watched too many movies of the Godfather whacking people.'

Papa grinned and placed his hand over mine.

'Just kidding, Felice. I like spirit in a man. But I had you going, right? Anyway, to finish the story: the family of the friend went to see your mate Alex, to hear his and his wife's side of things, and here we are.'

'What's it to you?' I asked.

'He's Italian. So is Melissa.'

'So is the Pope,' I said. 'Get to the point. It's a long way back home.'

'We need your services, Felice.'

'I'm booked out with accounting.'

'We already have an accountant.'

'Then let him help you. I'm flat out with my chicken place.'

'You helped Alex and Zoltan. We'd like you to help us, too. We're not big business. We can't afford flashy investment brokers like Rene Rivkin, not that we'd want to. He's a show-off, attracts too much attention, and works for the wrong crowd. That's not us. We'd rather deal with one of our own. A new Australian. A good, quiet family man.'

'I get it. How much cash are we talking about?'

'Depends. See, you pay half your orders in cash. So do all the other businesses we service. It's the nature of little shops, right?

Everyone pays in cash. Sometimes you don't have time to bank it, so you pay your bills with it. It adds up.'

'Only on your end,' I said. 'How many other shops do you sell chickens to? I don't see any feathers around here. Where do you keep them?'

Papa gave me a sad little smile.

'What do you know about broiler and roaster farming, Felice?'

'I cook them. I pictured happy chooks scratching dirt on some rundown old farm before you chop their heads off.'

'We've had our fair share of feathers and chicken shit, my friend. These days we keep them in massive barns, and they're not ours anymore. We're contract growers for the big processing plants. We get thirty-five cents a chook. We literally work for chicken feed.'

'What about my chickens? I pay two dollars apiece. Where do they come from?'

'Same place. Processor sells them back to us for seventy cents.'

'How many places like mine do you sell to?'

'A lot. We're a big family. Giorgio, Lorenzo, Riccardo, Alessandro, and that's just my boys. Then there are my three brothers' children and wives and grandchildren. Do you come from a big family, Felice?'

'Not that big, but it's growing. We need a bigger place to live. I'll help you with your investment problem if you help me grow my business. I don't ask for much. Just take my seasoning samples to every outlet on your books. It'll save me a lot of driving.'

20

Chasing calmer skies

A few weeks after my Italian meeting, the council health inspector paid me a visit. According to him, there'd been a complaint, by an undisclosed party, about an undisclosed issue. Which I took to mean: We've got nothing, but we'll turn over every tile until we do.

And they did. They found a loose floor tile, the bain-marie running under sixty degrees, and two rust spots on the handle of one of the chicken trolleys. I got slapped with an improvement notice. Andy scored a B minus for kitchen cleanliness, with a follow-up inspection booked in a month.

No big deal, until the inspector added, 'We'll take food samples then.'

That got me thinking. Was he being nice? Was it a warning? It started to play on my mind, just like that day at Curacao airport, when I ditched the toothpaste tube with the two joints inside on a hunch.

I know how Captain Cook must have felt when he wrote in his log book: September 2, 1769, by 4 p.m., crossing latitude 40°22′ South without spotting a scrap of land. The weather was brutal, gales, hail, squalls, sheets of rain. I'd planned to keep heading south as long as the westerlies held, even though the odds of finding *Terra Australis Incognita* looked grim. But the storm was too wild, dangerous enough to shred our sails and rigging. So I dropped the mainsail, rode her out under the foresail, and turned north. Better that than retracing our steps. We chased calmer skies, and bumped into New Zealand and Australia proper on a hunch. That's the irony of life.

I read too many sea-faring adventures to trust the wind. So I followed my hunch, swapped cannabis for okra, and never looked back.

Turns out I was still the lucky one.

Istvan and Alex, on the other hand, were not. They got raided by the police, not for the cannabis plantation in the backyard, not for the rebirthed cars. The cops came knocking on the trail of a tow truck company operating outside licensed zones to dodge costly inner-city fees. Never mind spray-painting hot cars or growing a field of pot, licensing fees got the boys in blue moving. And once they moved in, they called in a bloke with a shovel to do some digging behind the blackberry bushes.

No fine was issued. The case lingered, then fizzled out. Istvan married Maria, an Italian girl he met through Melissa. Clans stick together under the Australian sun. They moved away and started afresh. Janine and I went to their wedding, then dinner at their new suburban house. She was a brilliant cook, just like Melissa. That was the last time we saw them.

Alex was untouched by the excitement. His business kept ticking over. He started showing profits in his tax returns and handed over a new bag for deposit, twice a year. I got him to co-ordinate dates with Zoltan and Papa, so the bags turned into suitcases and rode in the Qantas cargo hold.

I still did a bit of writing on the side. Irana's note, "write your own", finally lit my fire. I remembered the stories I'd devoured as a young adult. All I had to do was tell them again, in my own voice, in the first person, and set them at sea, right next to where we lived on Western Port Bay.

I was *Robert der Fischer*, and Sauerländer let me moor my boat right at their publishing house. I didn't try hard, just wrote a story I would've liked to read growing up, and it turned out to be a success. It's the only book that ever netted me five figures. It had a print run of five thousand and went into second print soon after. It got translated into eight languages, went into paperback and picked up a few awards along the way. I wrote a few more YA stories that all got picked up, but I still made my living from seasoning chickens and banking for Papa and Zoltan.

One of the consequences of using a real setting for a fictional memoir, even if aimed at young readers, was that they would eventually be old enough to travel and go for a look-see themselves. My books did well in Germany. After a while, my publisher started forwarding fan mail from German readers that had followed my hero's path right to my doorstep. Had I used my Myers Road address, they probably would have knocked on the door and given Budgie another fright. Freaky.

About Budgie: when we moved back to Switzerland for a while, we handed him on to Janine's fellow teacher, Dorothy, and her husband, Bob Blanch. They lived in an old apple packing shed on an acreage and took horses on agistment. The shed-house was made of corrugated iron and looked like a giant Nissen hut, one room only, with a mishmash of furniture and carpets on trestles grouped into partitions.

Dot and Bob had lost their son in a car wreck, right at their front gate. They took in Budgie and made him their new son. He had free rein of the house, no walls to stop him wandering into the kitchen for a go at the butter dish, then gliding over to Bob on the other side, nibbling the head of his beer while they watched TV.

I missed my little margin bell ringer, but I was glad for the three of them, keeping each other company.

Our third child was delivered at the Hastings Bush Nursing Hospital, with the help of one of Janine's family friends, Dr Peter Rush. It was quite a party. Caesarean with a spinal block so Janine could enjoy the show for once. I stood at the end of the surgical table, hiding behind the viewfinder of my camera.

One of the party guests held the baby aloft like a trophy wrestled from the womb.

'Isn't she beautiful!' I said, clicking a few frames of a naked baby with great big purple balls.

We named her Michael David.

We'd done our bit for the human race, one for Mum, one for Dad, and a spare for Australia.

I guess I was happy with life just the way it now was. Business hummed along, writing finally produced some extra lunch money and the frequent flyer miles and cash deposits started to add up.

When life runs along smoothly, I get itchy feet. Mum always said it was a great failing of mine. She quickly changed her tune when I told her we were coming back for a while.

I didn't really need an excuse for the move, but I got one all the same: The Education Department of my home state invited me to do readings at primary schools. They targeted boys because they just wouldn't read as much as the girls. I think it was something like 60% to 40%. According to the Education Department, I was the chosen one to make it happen, at one hundred and ten francs a lesson plus expenses, which added up to more than I ever made in book royalties.

I sold the chicken bar and Melissa's recipe to another hopeful Colonel Sanders, and we flew back to Switzerland into the coldest of winters in 1986, cursing our decision walking through the snow-covered parking lot.

We got used to it: the half-hour ritual of wrapping three children in jumpers and coats, hats and gloves, just to walk to the park. And always, in the back of your mind, Australia, where housewives ducked out in dressing gowns to buy milk from the corner shop. Live in two countries and you can't help comparing them.

21

David and Goliath

Mum and Dad were over the moon. Dad had stocked up on chocolate bars and Mum had our kitchen on the first floor all set up.

We stayed at their place for a while, until we found our own house near the ice rink made immortal by The Who. Three stories, next to a park. Plenty of room, a big garden, a lawn that flowered in spring. Grape vines on the back veranda in summer, crushed into sour wine with our bare feet. A fireplace we paid for in winter, just to roast a chook.

The reading gig for the Education department lasted only a few weeks but it paid enough for a new family car. When it came to an end, I didn't quite know what to do next. We had enough money to live on for a while, so there was no pressing need to find work. I still kept checking out the job market section of Saturday's edition of the *Tages Anzeiger*.

Amidst all the big, flashy ads for accountants and office managers, I stumbled across a small, half-column, three-line notice written in English. It was looking for an accountant fluent in English and proficient in Swiss accounting and tax code. The company's name was printed in bold, no logo or any other embellishment: *USA TODAY International* Brandisstrasse 32, Zollikon, and a phone number.

I'd never heard of USA TODAY, the newspaper. I assumed it was some kind of import-export outfit. I wasn't exactly itching to take another job working for the man, but something about that minimalist approach tugged at me. Not the job itself, the mystery behind it.

Who placed the ad? Who was meant to read it? And what kind of operation needed someone fluent in both English and Swiss tax law, yet couldn't be bothered to mention salary, scope, or even a hint of what the role entailed?

Either the ad was written by someone who had no clue what they were hiring for, or they couldn't care less if anyone applied. Just the kind of dare that lights my fire.

I rang the number. A woman answered in a professional manner, in English, but with such a broad Bernese accent that I knew straight away she was Swiss. Her name was Vera Riva. She seemed surprised I was calling about the job.

'Come and see us tomorrow during office hours. We can talk then.'

No questions asked. No appointment necessary. Now I was really intrigued.

Brandisstrasse 32, Zollikon, on Zurich's Gold Coast, turned out to be a substantial three-story house with two large balconies, east and south, offering a multi-million-dollar view over Lake Zurich. The owner lived on the ground floor and rented out the two stories above, plus an extra-large, fully fitted loft under the roof.

USA TODAY had its Swiss branch office on the second floor and in the loft. There was no formal reception, not even a company name on the door, just a framed print of the first edition of USA TODAY hanging on the staircase wall to prove I was in the right place. Only now did I understand what USA TODAY was.

FOREVER DAY

The office had the layout of a domestic flat: one corridor, a small kitchen and utility room to the right, with offices branching off either side and a staircase leading up to the loft. At the end of the corridor, where the lounge would have been, there was one more large conference room, but I couldn't see in. The glass panel in the door had been taped over with newspaper.

Two or three young women worked in the offices, clearly clerical rather than editorial. Vera Riva high-heeled out of one of them to greet me. She was about my age, thin, well dressed, poised. I loved hearing that broad Bernese accent in a young woman. Mum spoke it just like that, but only with relatives from her side. With us, she stuck to Zurich dialect.

About the job,' said Vera Riva, 'you'll have to talk to Serena. She has all the details.'

'Okay. Is she in?'

'Oh no. Serena's in our London office.'

'Right. Look, I've no idea what you're doing here. Can you give me a rundown?'

'Certainly. Let's sit out on the balcony and have a chat.'

I followed her through the large middle office and out onto the balcony. There was a table and several chairs. The view hit me like a hammer. Homecoming. I was young me, looking out over the same lake from my bedroom window at the Hotel Lion, just a bit further up the road.

'How's your English?' Vera asked.

'Better than yours.'

'Good. You'll need it.'

'Did you place the ad?'

'Had to. David wanted to put an American accountant in charge, but he won't get a Swiss work permit unless we can prove we made every effort to find a local who could do the job.'

'Is that what the ad's all about? Did you write it? It really sucks.'

Vera laughed out loud. 'I like you, Flicks. I hope you get the job.'

'I'm not sure I want it. Why don't you just tell me what this is all about?'

'Sure. USA TODAY International is an offshoot of the American edition. Our paper is a condensed version, aimed at the international market, ex-pats, military, travellers. Our parent company is Gannett Media in Delaware. Our editorial office is in Washington. Our boss is David Mazzarella in New York. Our printer's Ringier in Adligenswil, and our accounts are kept by Gannett in Arlington, Virginia.'

'Bloody hell.'

'What we do here is liaise with Ringier. You know them, right?'

'I don't think there's a Swiss alive who doesn't read at least one of their publications.'

'They print us. On a new MAN offset press they bought and installed in Adligenswil, right next to *Blick*.'

FOREVER DAY

'You know *Blick* gave away one thousand free tickets for the Jimi Hendrix concert in '68?'

'I wouldn't mention that in your job interview. David's kind of old Boston school. Harvard and Red Sox, but definitely not Jimi Hendrix. You know, he made his career as a journalist covering the Vatican for the Associated Press'

'A good Catholic.'

'What was that?'

'Never mind. Go on.'

'As I said, we tell Ringier how many copies we need printed each night. The print run is the total that has to come off the press. The print distribution schedule shows how they must be bundled for pickup by the trucks and cars heading to the distribution centres. We also provide Ringier with the routing labels for every bundle.'

'Where do they go?'

'Everywhere. All over Europe and the Middle East. We charter a plane from Basel to London Stansted. The papers must reach Basel before 1 a.m., no commercial flights are allowed to depart after that. Once the plane lands, a local distributor handles delivery in the UK and transshipments to the Middle East. Our biggest distributor is FPS, a German company that also handles The Wall Street Journal. They pick up at the print site in one-ton Citroën rockets and make it to Paris and Frankfurt by 5 a.m.'

'Impressive. And you do it all here?'

'Right here. Still setting it up. Bit hectic sometimes. David's working on a new program to speed things up.'

FOREVER DAY

'David Mazzarella in New York?'

'Nah, David Sundwall-Byers. He's with Gannett. They made him General Manager for USA TODAY Europe.'

'Where is he?'

'Conference room.'

'The one taped over with newspaper?'

'That's him. Doesn't want to be disturbed. I'll introduce you when we're done. What else do you want to know?'

'Well, how do I fit into all this? I've got no clue about newspaper printing or circulation.'

'You'll be handling the accounts.'

'Where are they?'

'Downstairs, or you'll have to pick one of the empty offices up here.'

'Doing what?'

'Whatever accountants do. Paying Ringier, paying the distributors, paying our wages, sending invoices, keep the books for Gannett. All the boring stuff.'

'Who's doing all the boring stuff now? Who pays your wage?'

'Serena and Arthur Andersen Accounting.'

'Serena in London. Arthur Andersen where?'

'Zurich branch. One of their junior managers is upstairs.'

FOREVER DAY

'Doing what?'

'Dunno. The boring stuff.'

'Can I talk to him?'

'Go ahead. While you do that, I'll book your ticket to London for the interview. Tomorrow, 9 a.m. departure, sound good?'

'Sure. Wouldn't miss it for the world.'

I went upstairs into the loft. It was a very big room, white walls, exposed dark beams, and rafters from the roof structure. Furnished with just one desk and two giant hydroponic trees, which I later learned cost two hundred francs a month to maintain. Two gardeners came in weekly, dressed like they were about to plant a row of vegetables.

Between the trees sat the man from Arthur Andersen. Junior manager, fresh out of college, but better dressed than me. I looked around, hoping for a hidden computer or at least a filing cabinet. Nothing. Just a pile of ledgers on the desk and an adding machine with a strip of paper trailing to the floor like a bureaucratic tail.

We did the introductions. I asked what his job was. He said he kept the ABC records, copied from the sales figures, minus the returns. I had no idea what he meant.

He explained: the Audit Bureau of Circulations audits paid newspaper sales. If you send a hundred copies to a newsstand and they only sell fifty, the unsold ones get their mastheads ripped off and returned to the distributor. Those get deducted from the invoice.

For advertisers, the ABC-audited figure is the Holy Grail. The more copies you sell, the better the ad rates.

'Where do you get those figures from?' I asked. 'Who sends out the invoices and collects the returns?'

'Myrta gives them to me.'

'Myrta?'

'Downstairs. Tall, dark hair.'

'And what do you do with them?'

'I enter them into the ABC audit ledger.'

'That's it?'

'That's the job, yes.'

'Holy Mother of God. Who hired you?'

'Arthur Andersen.'

'I know you work for them. I mean, USA TODAY? Gannett?'

'Arthur Andersen in Richmond. London. They work for the UK office.'

'So let me get this straight: Serena in London hires Arthur Andersen in London who hires Arthur Andersen in Zurich to send you here to copy figures into a ledger. How many hours a week?'

'Forty. I'm in my second month.'

'What's your rate?'

'I don't think I'm at liberty to say. I don't know who you are.'

'By tomorrow I might be your new boss. Humour me. You must have some idea what they charge for your service.'

'Standard rate is two hundred francs an hour.'

'Holy insert, insert, insert, insert. Do me a favour, take that adding machine and calculate a yearly salary at that rate, based on two hundred and fifty eight-hour working days.'

'Don't need a calculator. Four hundred thousand francs.'

'You're quick. I'm sure you'll get another job.'

Vera was waiting for me downstairs.

'All done. You can pick up your ticket from the Swissair desk in Kloten. Business class, return flight at 2.30. You should make it back before rush hour. I'll put together an info package while you talk to David.'

She knocked on the conference room door and held it ajar, grinning.

'Wait for it,' she whispered.

After a pause, a voice called out: 'I know you're there, Vera. Make it quick!'

David Sundwall-Byers looked like my grade nine art teacher. Short, neatly trimmed beard, steel-rimmed glasses, and an ill-fitting but comfortable suit. He sat at a large conference table in front of an IBM PC.

Vera did the introduction. He shook my hand but didn't get up. We made small talk until he said:

'I like your accent.'

'Which one?'

'Both. I've never heard a Swiss speak English with an Australian accent.'

'Are you in charge of the office?' I asked.

'I guess I am, for now. Look, I'm not into the business side. I'm a circulation guy, Gannett sent me to set up a print distribution schedule we can run on a PC. I use Lotus 1-2-3. It's a killer with only 640 KB of RAM.'

'I've never worked with a PC or Lotus,' I said. 'My last company had an IBM mainframe. Why not use something bigger?'

'I'm not a computer guy either. This is what I use back home, so it'll have to do. By the way, there's a brand-new IBM Compact Mainframe downstairs. It's set up for accounting with a German ledger program we use back home. You'll be using that one if you get the job.'

In the corridor, Vera handed me a plastic bag with the big blue USA TODAY logo on the sides.

'I added some promo material from corporate,' she said. 'Have a good trip.'

'Wait, David said there's a computer downstairs? You've got more rooms down there?'

'Ah, that! Just the one by the stairs. That's where the boys from Gannett set it up. Come on, I'll show you.'

I followed her down to the next landing. It was a different setup to upstairs. From the stairs we stepped into a hall with one room to the left and a partition at the end, marked with a company logo on the office door.

FOREVER DAY

Vera opened the side room. The mainframe was just a small box, nothing like the monster we'd used in the dust-and-air-controlled room at the fireplace office.

'Neat,' I said. 'But I won't be working down here. Move it upstairs into the loft and sack the guy on four hundred K.'

'If you get the job.'

I went home and Janine asked me what I'd learned.

'It's a newspaper, owned by Goliath and run by two Davids. The job is the Virgin Mother of Accounting and I'm the chosen one to assist in the parthenogenetic birth. I'm off to London tomorrow. Chill the Champaign, Janine and get the nibblies ready. I feel a celebration coming on.'

22

Ode to Vera Riva

I didn't meet my new boss's boss, David Mazzarella, in the London office, even though I later learned that he was in the neighbourhood at the time. In fact, I wouldn't meet him for several more months. But I did meet two more Davids from circulation.

David Mile High, technically based in the Zurich office, happened to be in London that day for a meeting with the other circulation manager, David "Jonesy" Jones. That name sounds made up. It isn't. But to avoid conflict, I'll call him David Who.

I got to know David Who quite well over the next few years. We even met socially once or twice with our families. One day, he told me he was related to Pete Townshend from The Who. Uncle or something, close enough to stay over in the gatehouse or whatever it was on Pete's estate in the hills. It actually was just a stone's throw from the office; I could have walked up there and asked.

David Who was a straight kind of guy, not one to make up stories.

'You know, Pete's stone deaf,' he said, matter-of-factly.

Be that as it may, isn't it amazing how my life, his life, and probably the lives of our entire generation somehow, even if slightly, crossed paths with The Who?

The London office of USA TODAY was tucked into the swanky suburb of Richmond. perched above an antique shop. To get in, I had to ring a bell so someone could buzz me through the front door. A very long, very narrow, very English flight of stairs led up to the office. Honestly, it wasn't much better than a carpeted ramp in a chook house. These were the people who once built Windsor Castle! I looked up and groaned. I must have muttered something unflattering, because from upstairs I heard someone trying very hard not to burst out laughing.

Serena was waiting for me.

She showed me around and introduced the staff: Hugh Graham, head of circulation and office manager; Jonesy Who; Claire Southall from Classifieds; and one or two support staff. Serena wasn't what you'd call a senior figure, and she was clearly out of her comfort zone. She told me straight up, she'd never signed up for the job. It had been thrown at her during the first turbulent weeks of the adventure that became USA TODAY International.

She showed me how she compiled the profit and loss statements and the balance sheet. It looked kind of normal, until she explained that if she couldn't get the actuals, she'd just plug in the budgeted amounts. You don't have to be an accountant to know that's wishful thinking. Still, she was nice, and very upfront about it. In a court of law, it would probably count as a confession of fraud.

I started to wonder who the hell was going to employ me. Serena?

I looked at her across the desk. What to say?

She beat me to it.

'I had a talk with Vera and David,' she said. 'We think you fit the bill. Ah yes, the remuneration. What do you think about this figure as a starting salary?'

While she spoke, she wrote a number on a piece of paper and handed it to me.

I would have worked for less.

The interview was over in a flash. I stepped out of the office and walked along the busy street. The skies had darkened. I ducked into Marks & Sparks and bought myself a double-breasted trench coat with smooth lining, as befitted the Queen's Australian subject I was. Serena had given me a voucher for the taxi company they used. I preferred to hop into a black cab and be called "guv" all the way to Heathrow.

On the flight home I drank a couple of Bloody Marys, there wasn't time for more. It's just a hop and a skip from Heathrow to Kloten. While I enjoyed my British hour, I got thinking about what had just happened. Why send me all the way to London to accept a job they could have given me the day before? I was yet to learn that the American way of doing business is as simple and yet as complex as conducting a war.

In the arrival hall I passed a good-looking woman in a business suit with a jacket and matching skirt. We looked at each other with the flicker of recognition from a ghost past. Miriam, Bigi's chaperon.

'Flicks?'

We shook hands, as formal Swiss do. She looked me up and down in mocking appreciation.

'Look at you! They finally turned you,' she said with a trace of sadness.

FOREVER DAY

I sheepishly grinned and nodded. I didn't want to tell her that I was a chameleon.

I'd left the car home for Janine, we only had the one. The train was much more convenient: no parking hassles and just minutes to walk either end. I'd bought presents for Janine and the kids at Heathrow Airport. It set a costly precedent for a lot more trips to come.

I rang Vera from home.

'I'm glad you got the job,' she said. 'Make the boring stuff fun, I hope.'

'I know it was you, so thank you, Vera. What did it?'

'We had no clue we had a leech sitting under our roof on four hundred Ks. Not even David makes that much. Next time you find a scoop like that, put it in a memo, before somebody else takes credit.'

'You wouldn't do that, would you?'

'Not me, no. But somebody up the corporate ladder might. We have a lot of shadows, Flicks. When do you start?'

'Nobody asked me. Seeing that you're in charge, when do you want me?'

'Tomorrow eightish. We don't punch a clock.'

Let me just pause for a minute or two. Vera Riva, I was to learn, was a one-in-a-million woman who ever worked for the man. Impulsive like a rogue balloon. A quirky dresser. A connoisseur of the finer things, self-assured beyond belief, I never had a thing for her, but I came to love her to bits.

FOREVER DAY

I didn't know much about Vera's work history. She came from an ad agency. USA TODAY hired her first. She found the office in Zollikon and set it up. Functional IKEA furniture. Coffee maker from JURA, Swiss-made, reliable, unmatched.

She built the place. The rest of us showed up later.

She poached the best from her former employer, Myrta, who was to work for me.

Vera had a magic wand I never saw. You'd ask for anything, and it was done.

On Fridays, she'd bring out a bottle of wine and make us sit on the balcony. TGIF, she'd say, Thank God it's Friday.

I only ever got a glimpse of her personal life. Not married, but involved with a boyfriend who sold printing presses around the globe. Ringier, printing press, that's how USA TODAY got onto her. I can't recall his name, but he drove seriously powerful cars. Vera sometimes borrowed one to drive to work, parked a spectacularly beautiful Lamborghini right next to my boring old family car.

She was the most incredible woman I ever worked with. And yet, somehow, she was never put in charge. Still don't get it.

By the time I showed up, the computer had been moved upstairs. It was working fine, so I started digging. The accounts were there, but empty. Every single entry was just a random number the techs had used to test the system. I added my own, just to see it run. I could print ten different statements, and each one showed as little as Alex's panel beating shop. My joke to Janine had come true: Virgin Books.

FOREVER DAY

The only report with numbers in it was the budget. No surprise there. When you set up a business, you don't have actuals. You have projections, wishful thinking, a mirage. It applied to my chicken business as much as to USA TODAY. They just had a much richer daddy to help them along.

Soon enough, I had those books bubbling like Melissa's Chicken Paprikash. The secret spice? Intercompany account. That's where corporate charges you for your promotional mugs. That's where you send them a windfall that never lands in your accounts. That's where you tuck Papa's money and have Zoltan take it out. Traceable nothing.

Make the boring stuff fun and profitable. Nobody ever caught on.

A few months into the job, I made a list of things I wanted changed. We were all drowning in administrative work. My local boss, David Sundwall-Byers, was a brilliant circulation guy; his only goal was to sell more papers. Everything else was the boring stuff.

At the time, we had seven bodies selling and only four making it work. David had hinted, more than once, that he was just about done. He was a family man, married to a practicing medical doctor, with a flock of children somewhere in rural Texas, I believe.

I went to see him without much hope. He made me sit down and go through the list, line by line. When we finished, he stood up, shook my hand, and said:

'Good luck with it, Flicks. I'm done.'

FOREVER DAY

And just like that, I was put in charge. USA TODAY International. Director of Finance and Operations, Europe and Middle East. I kid you not. It barely fit on the business card Vera had ready within a day. I hardly ever showed it to anyone. I still think of it as a joke.

David Mazzarella didn't think so. He jetted in to confirm my new role and gave me a fifty percent raise. He never lingered at the Country Club. I usually met him at his hotel, the legendary Waldhaus Dolder, perched in the hills above the city, with lake and mountain views, and close enough to the forest and the Zurich Zoo to hear elephants trumpeting at dusk.

Mazzarella looked as Italian as his name suggested. I could imagine him fitting right in with the Papal crowd, sombre, reserved, not one for jokes or fun. I never learned much about his personal life. For all I know, he never had children. But when he visited our home, he was the nice Italian uncle who played with ours.

He built quite a career as editor of USA TODAY after I left, and eventually wrote a cookbook filled with memories and recipes from his centenarian Italian mother. I wish he'd shared those with me back then.

He was the opposite of his boss, Al Neuharth, and for that reason alone, I'm grateful.

I never knew when he was in town until he'd call for a dinner meeting at the Waldhaus. 'Nothing fancy,' he'd say. 'Just informal dress.'

I'd show up in an open-neck shirt, only to be stopped at the dining room door. They had plenty of ties to loan. Informal, for

FOREVER DAY

David, meant a blue blazer and a roll-neck top, neither of which could bloody well accommodate a tie.

He always made me bring the latest financials, but insisted I keep the printout in my lap, under the table. You didn't do business in the dining room of the Waldhaus. That kind of guy.

My official title might've been a farce, but the job certainly wasn't. I'd hired a few more people to run the accounts. I still did the reports and the monthly close myself to keep Papa out of the loop, but most of my time was now taken up with what the job actually was: Publishing Manager. That's how it was entered in the official register of commerce. USA TODAY International Inc, New York, Zollikon branch. Publishing Manager with sole signatory power.

I could've sold the whole shop right under corporate's nose with the stroke of a sharpie. Legally. But I was never quite that big a crook.

Keeping the printing press rolling wasn't my job. Keeping the cars with the bundles of papers on the road wasn't my job either. But who do you think they rang in the middle of the night when things went wrong? The Publishing Manager.

I should've kept a call log. Some of it was tragic, some of it was funny, all of it had to be dealt with, day and night.

Our German distributor had a driver who broke the 130 km/h limit near Basel by 40 km or more on a daily basis. The automatic speed check lit up like a Christmas tree until the cops finally set a trap and took him in. And guess who they called? I had to arrange bail before breakfast.

FOREVER DAY

Basel Airport had me on speed dial. I lost count of how many times they rang in the middle of the night, asking where our car was. The window for takeoff was closing fast. They were kind enough to grant us an extension, at their discretion, when things got too tight.

Ringier had two point-persons to liaise with us. It gave us a buffer, but when things went wrong, the knock-on effect rattled all the way to New York and Washington.

The funny ones were the walk-ins, people who thought we actually ran the paper from our office, with a newsroom and a printing press tucked behind the coat rack. They just waltzed in. We had no security at all. Some were curious to see who made their paper. Others had a story they needed published at all costs.

One of them asked to use our toilet and never came out. Vera was ready to call the cops, but our young subscription manager fetched a crowbar from his car and jimmied the door. She hadn't fainted. She was just as confused as the story she'd tried to sell us.

Not my job? Everything on home soil was my job.

23

David Mile High

David "Mile High" was never my responsibility. He belonged to Circulation and should technically have been stationed in the London office, or in the Bahamas, if he'd had his way. His name wasn't really Mile High, but as it was almost the first thing he told me, I labelled him thus.

'Hi, I'm David insert, insert. I'm the Circulation Manager. In my spare time I fly planes, and I'm a member of the Mile High Club.'

Smoothest pick-up line I've heard thus far.

He was Swiss, with Scottish parents, and spoke both languages without accent. Some English, too. I have to admit, he was tall, good-looking, and almost on par with that other Scotsman, Sean Connery.

The circulation manager was entitled to a company-leased car. He chose a top-range Audi that exceeded the budget limit. I deducted the difference from his monthly salary. More work for me, less money for him. No wonder we didn't get on.

He insisted the car be fitted with a mobile phone. Handheld models weren't available back then. His mobile consisted of two large bricks, one for power, one for signal, that could be plugged into the car or carried by hand, assuming both hands were free.

Next, he needed a personal assistant. Not for scheduling or admin, but so he could ring and inform her he was fifteen minutes out from touchdown at home base. Her name was Jennie, a Kiwi. Blonde, married, and a livewire. She and her husband liked planes, not to make out in, but to jump out of. They were active members of a formation skydiving team. No time for children, just heads-down at terminal velocity, holding hands. Not my idea of a romantic date.

Jennie's position wasn't in the budget, but David somehow got the nod to hire her from his boss in London. He was on the road a lot, checking newsstands all over the place, mostly in picturesque, sunny locations like North Africa or the French Riviera. His expense reimbursement forms were like puzzle books. Where's Wally? Elisabeth from Accounts was the editor with the red pencil. She got a lot of enjoyment out of finding Wally.

David must have taken his entire wardrobe on the road and had it hotel-laundered. Every meal he claimed came with a spare bottle or a packet of cigarettes. Parking tickets had fines attached. Hotel barber visits were so numerous that Elisabeth suspected it was code for massage. I let her deal with it. She was worth her mob of curls in gold.

She'd answered an ad Vera placed for me, looking for an accounts person. Vera showed her into my office and made a thumbs-up sign behind her back before closing the door. I hired her on the spot, just because I liked her pluck. She hadn't done any real accounting work; her last job was managing a fashion boutique in Davos. I never hired anyone for their résumé alone.

Anyway, she turned out to be a gem. A great eye for detail and a steady hand driving through the fog. Not a cheap gag. She actually married a fog chaser with a degree from ETH Zurich, one of the world's leading universities for science and technology. There really was such a thing.

FOREVER DAY

I went to their wedding in the church. His fellow fog chasers lined the stairs to form an archway with hand-held fog detectors and fog horns.

Back to David's assistant, Jennie. She was bored out of her mind. David had her ring around setting up meetings, only for London to change it all. Because David was hardly ever in the office and she had nothing else to do, she helped out Myrta with the daily print run schedule. She was so good at it that I rang David's boss, Hugh, in London and told him Jennie had quit and I'd re-hired her on the spot. I said she'd still answer David's phone. I think Hugh got the message.

David really did have a license to pilot a single-engine plane. He never had any money, so when he ran out of time to log his required flying hours; he tried to talk us into chipping in to hire a Cessna for a sightseeing tour. I don't think anyone in the office ever took the bait.

Jennie had a love affair with Auntie Ju, a Junkers JU52 tri-engine transport plane with a corrugated aluminium fuselage. A German relic from between the wars. Three of them were still operational in Switzerland, based at the Swiss Air Force airport in Zurich Dübendorf, run by a private company offering sightseeing tours. They flew low and slow, with a distinctive piston-engine-propeller sound. Jennie was from the same village I lived in with my family. Auntie Ju was a familiar feature in our skies.

Jennie's skydiving club had a gentleman's agreement with the JU52 operator, who was required to regularly perform flight performance tests with different payloads. The prescribed method was to fill large barrels with water, do the test, pour some water out, and repeat. Apparently it was awkward and time-consuming, especially when the loads had to be shifted around the cargo hold.

People were easier to move. And easier to dispose of, by simply jumping out of the plane. Jennie's skydiving mob got a package deal, and she and her husband were on speed dial. I believe they were part of an international group of formation skydivers who temporarily held the record for the number of bodies holding hands while speeding toward the ground.

Jennie left USA TODAY before I did. She and her husband returned to New Zealand to jump out of planes on the opposite side of the world. The JU52s kept making their slow way across Swiss skies for another eighteen years. Back in Australia, I was devastated to learn that one of the three planes had crashed in the mountains on a sightseeing tour, killing all twenty passengers and crew. It spelt the end for Auntie Ju.

24

Call Me Al

Al Neuharth was a newspaper man from the word go. He eventually ended up as chairman of Gannett with a hundred papers and scores of TV and radio stations. He settled in Cocoa Beach, Florida in a ten-thousand-square-foot mansion with eleven bedrooms and twelve bathrooms. The property was known as Pumpkin Centre but he and David Mazzarella always referred to it as Al's log cabin. They also referred to our Zollikon office as their Country Club.

Later on, Al walked into our Country Club for a coffee. He had Vera show him the JURA coffee maker it was made with.

'I'll have two of those,' he said. Machines, not coffee.

'Certainly, Mr Neuharth,' Vera said in her crisp Bernese tone.

'You can call me Al.'

It was shortly after Paul Simon's earworm hit the charts. *You can call me Al.* From that moment on, we only referred to the chairman as Call Me Al.

Vera had the two machines delivered to the office in no time. She got the FedEx guy in to pick them up. Then, silence. No word from the Americans.

And here comes the indisputable proof that I didn't make this up: they couldn't read the German instructions and they didn't run on 220 Volts. JURA had no English version at the time. Normal people, like us, would've just found a translator.

Not Call Me Al's mob.

FOREVER DAY

They seriously asked me to contact JURA and propose a deal: we'd arrange to print an English version if JURA agreed to buy it from us. That was the pitch. If there was a buck to be made from printing, Call Me Al's office was in it, no matter how outlandishly stupid the whole thing was.

Back at Pumpkin Center Resort, the powerful outdoor lighting interfered with the nesting habits of sea turtles, whose hatchlings rely on moonlight to navigate. Cocoa Beach officials complained in vain. Al Neuharth's larger-than-life persona found it necessary to light up the beach like a newsroom, even if the turtles couldn't find their way home.

The turtles eventually got their revenge.

After Neuharth's death, the property was sold to be turned into a wedding venue. During construction, it burned to the ground. Smoke on the water. A fire in the sky. Deep Purple didn't write a song about Al's cabin, so nobody cared.

Despite his flamboyance and overblown ego, Call Me Al was a shrewd newspaper man with a vision that, back in '80s, was almost unthinkable: a truly nationwide American newspaper, in colour, printed simultaneously at multiple sites. It required a massive investment in satellite technology, something no one had attempted before.

Once he had the USA covered, he went global. Same technology, same bravado. The first international newspaper satellite dish was installed on the roof of the Ringier print site in Adligenswil, near Lucerne. From Pumpkin Center to Adligenswil, the signal was clear: Think Big. Print Bigger.

The technology was amazing, yet simple. Editorial assembled the paper, each page laid out on a large film and faxed to Adligenswil. I seem to recall it took a few detours en route, zigzagging across the U.S. to reach the beam-up station on the West Coast.

From there: up to the satellite, down to Adligenswil. Not pinpoint microwave precision back then, the signal footprint was wide enough to blanket a good chunk of Europe.

Once received by the computer at Ringier's, the system sent it back for confirmation. What had been sent had to return. Only then was the film printed and turned into a traditional metal print plate for the offset press: one for black, three for colour.

It was a marriage of printing tradition and space-age technology. A dance between continents, American satellite marvel, German engineering and Swiss precision printing. No wonder it worked.

I never was, nor wanted to be, remotely like Al. I would have turned the lights off for the turtles, and I definitely wouldn't have needed more bathrooms than bedrooms. But one thing we had in common: we both liked writing. Maybe, buried beneath his show-off persona, there was a humble hack? I doubt it. He had to turn every aspect of his life into a transaction with everybody watching on. After he published his Buscapade book, he boasted that he made his employees pay for it.

Buscapade was his idea of taking the newsroom on the road, interviewing governors and assorted dignitaries in every American state. But of course, he had to do one better. Jetcapade followed. He'd cover the world in a Gulfstream jet, the blue logo emblazoned on the side, showing them how things were done in the good old U.S. of A.

When Al did Switzerland, one of Al's two pilots showed up in my office and asked me for a job. He wanted to fly our delivery

FOREVER DAY

Learjet to Stansted to clock up hours needed to pilot a DC9. I'm a seafarer at heart so I don't care if it's true, but obviously flying our kind of twin engine paper-delivery jet was comparable to piloting a DC9. I must have answered two or more calls from other hopefuls over time.

While he was there, he dished the dirt on Al. Apparently, he had to stock the plane's fridge with three bottles of a specific brand of Finish vodka, nibblies, a fruit platter tailored exactly to Al's taste, and paper napkins cut to the specified size. I'll take any oath that this was fact. Al's people, through David, had me fax his comfort-wish list to some hotel later on. The boy who had started selling papers on the streets had become a man who'd long lost his grip on reality.

I have to admit, though. His excesses make a great story to tell.

During his Jetcapade reporting, Al stayed at the Dolder Waldhaus with his considerable entourage. They took up an entire wing of the building. Each morning, Al would jog through the woods toward the Zoo. He had a female bodyguard with him. Some robust woman, she was.

Al didn't strike me as a physical guy, and I believe he knew it. But he wanted to hide it. So instead of jogging side by side, he made his bodyguard stay behind him, creating the illusion that this muscular woman was struggling to keep up with Big Al. You get the picture.

Here's the thing: first, who in those woods around the Zurich Zoo would have even known who Al was, let alone wanted to jump him?

FOREVER DAY

Second, and more to the point, if I had hated him enough to take him out (which, of course, I didn't), I could have shouldered my Swiss army-issued assault rifle, kept in the attic with twenty-four rounds in a tin can, strolled into the woods, and shot him point blank from the front, with his bodyguard still trying to catch up.

And here's what I believe to be one hundred percent true: me walking through a Swiss forest with an army rifle slung over my shoulder probably would have attracted less attention than Al jogging with a bodyguard.

To stay with the military setting: David Mazarella was Al's aide-de-camp. Al would toss out a headline grabber, and David had to fill in the blanks, finish the sentence, so to speak. I fully acknowledge that Al was good at what he did. But strip away the job and the constant theatre, and one-to-one, as a human being, he never impressed me at all.

Janine and I were invited to join him for lunch at the Dolder. Shortly before his Swiss stop on Jetcapade, he'd interviewed the Pope. Janine had been in the Vatican on her European trip and was dying to hear about the encounter.

Al wore a whopper of a dress ring; Janine reckoned it was bigger than the Pope's. She would have loved to know if they'd compared rings. Or talked about the weather. Or anything normal humans talk about.

I saw a picture of the meeting: the Holy Father speaking to Al, who was holding a copy of USA TODAY, carefully angled to show the masthead with its blue logo. Clearly rehearsed. At the very least, he could have boasted about using the Pope for a clever promotional trick.

FOREVER DAY

Nothing.

Here was the man who'd met the world's elite, and not a single anecdote. Not even a funny sideline. On the drive home, Janine turned to me, still dazed by the silence, and said, 'What a boring old fart.'

My forever woman knows her men.

Anyway, Al did a bit of talking to me, all about his stay.

'When do I get my paper? 0400 hours, right?'

'I know the Zurich distribution finishes before then, so they should be at the hotel in time.'

'You'd better make sure.'

'No worries, she'll be right.'

On the way out, David came rushing after us. Pulled me aside and handed me a folded newspaper.

'You know he means it,' he said. 'You go to the print site and pick out three perfect copies. No scuff marks or streaks, no pressure lines or indentations. Folded like the one I just gave you. Put them in one of our promo bags and hang it on the outside door handle of room 7. Al gets up early. If his papers aren't there, you've got no job. Got it?'

'No worries, David.'

Right then and there, he didn't know it, but he'd lost his Swiss Publishing Manager. It wasn't a Fuck-you-Al moment, it just planted the seed.

FOREVER DAY

I only spoke to Al once more, a bit later, on a Sunday at home. One of his people rang and told me to hold for Al. I could hear a lot of people talking in the background, but eventually Al came on the line.

'I'm going into a bunker in a minute,' he said. 'We're doing a photo shoot with the civil defence guys in Zurich, for a piece about defended neutrality. Can you hop along in full uniform and gun, with a few of your army friends?'

'I'm not allowed to, Al,' I lied. 'Wearing a uniform off duty is an offense.' It was just a stab in the dark, but it worked.

'Don't want to rock the boat,' said Al.

It must be the most humble remark he ever made.

Humble Al? The man bigger than life, even in death?

Al Neuharth didn't just leave the stage, he required three curtains to fall. One was never going to be enough. Even in death, he remained a syndicate of multiple selves.

The first farewell was in Cocoa Beach, Florida, where he had spent his final years. Family, close friends, and a few old newsroom hands gathered under the sun with the sea turtles watching on. It was the kind of send-off that suggested a man at rest, though no one quite believed he'd stay that way.

The second was in Washington, D.C. Here, the tributes were formal. Senators, editors, and media executives lined up to remember the man who had redrawn the map of American journalism. It was a state funeral in all but name, a final press run for a man who had always known how to make and stay in the news.

FOREVER DAY

The third was in South Dakota, where it had all begun with his German parents. Windswept prairies, Lutheran hymns, and the long memory of a boy who sold newspapers during the Depression and never stopped believing in the power of print. They buried him in the soil that shaped him, but even there, the myth refused to settle. He had already etched himself into the landscape with foundations, scholarships for a state that had always been too small to hold him till his final rest.

Al had written the script for his demise well in advance. Ordinary men just die.

I doubt the enormous bill for Jetcapade was worth it from a journalistic point of view. Thirty-two countries on six continents in eight months. The team managed to line up at least one interview with a senior figure of state, plus assorted dignitaries and captains of industry.

Al's people wanted a picture of a Swiss banker in front of his bank. They rang me for advice. I told them to go for one of the smaller players; big banks didn't need USA TODAY's help to access American funds. I was suitably impressed when they managed to get the president of Julius Baer to pose inside the vault of the sixth-biggest Swiss bank.

As for the interviews with the 'common' people and whoever they thought mattered: it was all pre-written back home by an army of staffers and their preconceptions of what made a country tick. Once again, it was just another picture opportunity to showcase Big Al, sitting by the window of the USA TODAY Gulfstream IV, typing his state of 32 nations on a 1926 Royal typewriter.

FOREVER DAY

Al Neuharth. The American dream. Paperboy from poor German parents, turned publishing mogul and superstar showman at heart.

I would have loved to ask him: did he ever feel content just being Al? Did he ever tell anybody his true feelings, his shortcomings? Nobody can be a human having none.

Apart from the Swiss leg of the journey, I had very little to do with the jet-setting crowd, aside from being their paperboy on occasion, after the articles were published in the U.S. We never covered Jetcapade in the International edition, so as not to offend international diplomacy.

David instead FedExed me domestic newspapers he wanted delivered to some of the people or institutions featured in the articles. Most of it was routine forwarding work. But one request stuck in my mind: his insistence that I board a plane and hand-deliver twenty copies to the Kremlin.

I told him I wasn't going to knock on the Kremlin door. Ever. Besides, you couldn't just hop on a plane; visas took time to be approved.

'Al wants it done by tomorrow,' he said, not repeating his threat of a sacking but implying it all the same.

To me, William Tell. Too late, bailiff Gessler, I can only shoot the apple once. Had I missed, the second bolt of my crossbow was aimed right at your heart.

I would never go to Russia, even if I could. But I had a contact there: Peter, I've forgotten his last name. He worked for the Russian press agency Novostni. I can't recall where I first met him, probably at Ringier's, but he visited our Zollikon office a few times and came to my home, bringing presents for our children: wind-up tin toy animals that looked like they were made in the 1920s.

For whatever reason, he liked to keep in touch. Vera reckoned he was a spy for the KGB and flirted with him something dreadful. I don't know why. Maybe she just liked living dangerously.

Anyway, Peter was happy to help. I FedExed Al's papers to him at Novostni, and they made the Kremlin, two days late.

25

Snipers in the bushes

At the end of the '80s, I got a call from one of our many shadows at corporate. Our paper was probably one of the smallest and certainly the most unprofitable in the Gannett stable, but we were their golden gate to Heidiland. Every second executive used that as an excuse for a look-see, checking the books, checking the coffee maker, checking the system. I saw them all: dark blue suits, red ties, and one cashmere coat that Vera swore they passed from man to man.

They never lingered. They parked their rental Merc beside Vera's Lamborghini, visibly deflated. After a coffee or two and a conversation, usually about nothing in particular, sometimes about the Alps, they'd take off to tour the print site and the mountains. A few days later, on their way back, they'd call to say goodbye and ask me to write a report or a feasibility study, something to justify the trip. And I, being Janine's husband, Janine, who never sent the Jehovah's Witnesses down the long driveway without their twenty cents, complied. I could cook a good story from a dead fish, and losing money in the millions, I'd mastered the art of making it sound like a success.

This call wasn't from one of the mid-rank pests at corporate. No, this was about the motherload, the full infestation, gathering at the Bürgenstock resort in the hills above Lucerne for a Gannett board meeting. One of their number was Rosalynn Carter, wife of the former American president.

I'd heard whispers during one of my twice-weekly pilgrimages to the print site. I didn't take much notice. I worked in the real world, keeping things going. I didn't have time to worry about the high end of town. This was Gannett's do. No visit to Zollikon was planned; Ringier on the other hand was to get the full treatment.

That first phone call was weird enough. Gannett had rented the entire Bürgenstock Resort, three hotels, top to bottom. They flew in their own staff, their own equipment, their own everything. And then realised their PCs would fry if they plugged them into 220 volts.

So they called me.

I didn't know the guy. One of Al's people. I can't give you a verbatim account after all this time, but it went something like this:

'Al wants you to call IBM and get them to make our PCs work.'

'You can't be serious. IBM would die laughing if I called them. We've got one small computer and a few PCs from them, that's all.'

'You call them and tell them to come if they don't want to read in tomorrow's edition, with five million readers, that IBM is shit.'

Vera waved her magic wand and it was done. No embarrassment calling IBM, the maintenance crew at the Bürgenstock had it all under control.

The second call from the Bürgenstock mob was even weirder. To this day, I don't know what it was really about. All I can tell you is that it happened.

FOREVER DAY

This other Gannett guy rings and asks me where he can get a helicopter with twin engines. Me. Captain Cook. Apparently, one of their board, presumably Rosalynn Carter, would only fly in a twin-engine machine for safety reasons. And none were available in Switzerland. Not one.

I didn't bother asking Vera. She could've sourced a whole fleet of twin-engine choppers, armed or unarmed, and definitely equipped with a wine fridge for TGIF. But I let it go.

Later, David Mazzarella told me it really was the case; someone from Gannett had hired a twin-engine helicopter from Germany. He reckoned it just sat there on the helipad, unused.

There was no more immediate drama rolling down the slopes of the Bürgenstock in my direction. Ringier was closer, and they copped it. The Gannett board paid a visit to the print site. I wasn't invited. But years later, Michael Ringier wrote a piece about that memorable day:

"At the end of the eighties, it was a sight that had never been seen in Canton Lucerne. Twenty-five black limousines approached the Adligenswil printing plant in single file, and those who took a closer look at the environs spotted suspicious movements in the bushes surrounding the industrial estate: snipers and security guards were tokens of the highest level of US security. After all, the wife of former President Jimmy Carter was paying a visit to what was then Europe's only printing plant with a satellite aerial on its roof."

Our office copped a bit of shrapnel from the big do. David dropped by unannounced, trailing a middle-aged woman he introduced as Al's interior designer. On the way out, he leaned in and whispered: 'Girlfriend.'

FOREVER DAY

I don't retain a clear picture of her, but I remember she made a beeline for Vera, who, incidentally, dressed and looked far more like a real interior designer. Al's interior designer couldn't get the JURA coffee makers going. Vera showed her ours, which worked, and they got talking over coffee.

Apparently, the poor woman had suffered a bad encounter with nature, stranded on top of the Alps during a sightseeing flight. The heli tour operator had to ditch her to fly a quick rescue mission. No danger, and she wasn't alone, but it rattled her enough to require a shopping trip to Nice in Al's jet. The pilots were already sitting idle at the airport.

She was hell-bent on taking Vera along. Vera spoke excellent French and had the right look. I don't know how she got out of it, but I'm not surprised.

Sometime later, probably in one of Al's books, I saw the girl-friend's artwork in his office. From memory, it looked like a washing line with clothes pegs.

26

Locked and Loaded

Inevitably, the Swiss army caught up with me. They kitted me out for a refresher course, no way out. I wasn't thrilled. I hate authority in any form, but if it's part of one's civic duty, one just has to grin and bear it.

I didn't exactly have a stellar career in the army. I flunked out three-quarters through my first round with the mechanized infantry. A stroke of luck during house-to-house combat training: I jumped out of a second-storey window and couldn't get up. They carted me back to base. I couldn't move for a day or two, then they sent me home for medical tests. Turns out my back had suffered damage from Scheuermann's disease, contracted in my youth. Hippy hurray.

Not so fast, young recruit. You won't have to schlep heavy gear, but you can still work a typewriter, right? Bloody Ritchie Blackmore's ten-finger job came back to haunt me.

Because I'd gone over the required days of service, they said I'd earned the right to keep my semi-automatic SIG assault rifle. I didn't bloody want it, but it was considered honorary. During my first refresher, working in the office, a sergeant noticed my dusty gun sitting forlorn in the corridor gun rack. He tracked me down and ordered me to take it apart for inspection.

I hadn't used a gun for several years. I'd forgotten how. He didn't believe me, so he sat down and watched me try. Eventually, I managed to take it apart. He checked the bore with a little mirror. Turns out there was serious rust inside the barrel.

FOREVER DAY

My captain was a decent fellow. He went out of his way to get me a pistol instead of the rifle, but to no avail. Only end-of-service-age could us part.

By now I was close to forty. Janine jokingly called me and her friend's husband, Freddy, the two oldest privates in the Swiss army. I was only half a private, or an auxiliary private, if that's even a word.

Because I'd missed a couple of refreshers, I was reassigned to a new mechanised medical transport unit. It featured women drivers, which was a nice change, but I never got to see them. I was to be the girl-Friday typist for the Swiss equivalent of a two-star general. In civilian life, he was a gynaecologist.

I might be treading on thin ice here, but is it possible his day job was the reason he was such an utter asshole in the army? I mean, the Swiss army is made up of ordinary blokes who treat the service as a little holiday away from routine. Dad's Army. You don't need a little gynaecologist prick making you snap to attention and report in every time he enters the office, right?

After two or three days, he made everyone jump into trucks and relocate HQ to a bunker beneath a schoolhouse whose pupils were away on holiday. It was one of those emergency evacuation spiels, our kit bags had to stay behind, and we were only allowed to grab a couple of things before being whisked away. And just by the by, I had to load the office's two telex machines into the truck. No heavy lifting? Those things weighed a lot more than a machine gun mount!

I stayed incarcerated in that bunker for over a week, typing the storyboard script for his little war games before I saw daylight again. I had only one set of underpants and turned it every which way for seven days.

Things in the bunker office didn't improve, but the field kitchen had relocated and I was allowed out for lunch at the nearby pub. I rang Vera and cried a bit, so she set up a meeting and got some papers ready for me to sign. She showed up the next day with most of the girls from the office: Vera, Myrta, Elizabeth, Jennie, and the pretty junior accounts clerk whose name escapes me. Vera had reserved a table at the back and ordered the best the pub's kitchen, or anyone in the world, for that matter, could muster: a Bernese plate, a carnivore's fever dream of separately cooked meats, beef tongue, smoked pork loin, smoked bacon, pork knuckle, and the mother of all sausages, Bernese Saucisson. This was flanked by juniper-scented sauerkraut, air-dried and re-hydrated green beans, and potatoes.

The girls hardly touched their plates.

It occurred to me that Vera had staged a perfect tableau: an opulent meat-lover's feast for King Henry, flanked by the court's butterflies. Or perhaps it was a condemned man's last meal, fare-welled by his grieving family before being led back to his cell.

She was perfectly capable of both.

Back in the cell, the two-star gynaecologist was scouting out another war game, in concert with fighting units that would supply the victims to be transported by our unit. He was in the field a lot, which was a blessing, but I had to sleep right next to the phone. He'd call to announce his return with other officers and have me rustle up a midnight snack for the lot of them. With the kitchen gone, I had to walk all the way to the station or the servo for supplies.

FOREVER DAY

Girl Friday. Auxiliary private F'n F.

We all got base leave for two nights before the war game started. I ran a few extra copies of the war-game storyboard script through the spirit duplicator and exchanged them for free drinks with the lads. We were the best prepared unit and earned a meritorious mention. The little prick lapped it all up.

I can't even begin to describe the feeling of joy I got from handing back my army garb when I finally left Switzerland for good. The guy at the supply depot checked my gear and took my gun.

'We'll look after it for you until you come back,' he said, with a malicious grin.

I wonder if he's still there, waiting.

27

On the home front

Janine had long settled in by now. With the children at school, she had a bit more breathing space. Just when things were going smoothly, her mother died. She flew over for the funeral with the children and stayed a while.

When she came back, I noticed a slight change. She must have thought about our future, about what it meant to raise a family in what was still, and would always remain, a foreign land.

I wasn't as good a husband as I wanted to be, commuting to the print site, shuttling between Zollikon and the new London office, jetting off on a boss's errand, sometimes with a side trip down under. But that line of business was nearing its end. Papa had all but banked the family's treasure, and Melissa's kids had reached high school and driving age. There was no more surplus cash to be had.

I was to learn that lesson myself, soon enough.

With the Zollikon office humming and the London branch relocated from the Richmond antique shop to more professional quarters in High Holborn, David began looking further afield for my services. We now printed in Hong Kong and Singapore, though our Asian office wasn't in either city. It operated out of the Pacific Daily News office in Guam.

By then, David had hired a controller for his New York office, Barbara Krasne. She came with Time magazine credentials and was, technically, my new boss. In practice, little changed. I now spoke to her instead of David. She was kind, generous, and decidedly easier to get along with than her predecessor.

FOREVER DAY

David wanted me to move the family to Hong Kong to get an office going. We already had a couple of rooms set up for circulation, but no one in admin. Same old story. Newspaper guys operate like generals going to war; first they secure a printing bridgehead, then send in the circulation elite to conquer the ground. The grunts in admin come last.

This grunt talked it over with Janine. She was hesitant at first, but a change of scenery sounded exciting. Hong Kong was fine by her, provided we could find a comparable home. And that's where the buck stopped. Suitable apartments were just about on par with Fifth Avenue prices and David didn't feel too generous right then.

Instead, I was sent to Guam to meet up with Barbara Krasne and take an inventory. It was a proper mess, a lot worse than Zollikon on my first day. Barbara left me to it, counting the boxes and having them shipped to Zurich for evaluation. I ended up burning three carloads of it at the local waste incinerator plant that heated my hometown. The irony was not lost on me.

I had Circulation place an ad in the *South China Morning Post* for an accountant-office manager. I shortlisted eight promising candidates from their résumés, took the red-eye to Hong Kong, and went straight to the office to interview the lot. By the last one, I was more or less asleep, but I had my pick, the one I thought would fit the job.

I brought him to the Zollikon office and showed him how to run a similar setup. I had it all in writing. David had us compile folders of job descriptions early on, just in case he sacked one of us, so he could hand our obituaries to the next guy. Very much like the cashmere coat that went from visitor to visitor at corporate.

FOREVER DAY

It was exactly that kind of feeling that made me vow never to work for the man. You're never on firm ground if you're not in charge of yourself. No matter your place in the pecking order, if the food chain runs dry, you all suffer the same fate. The seed David an Al planted at the Dolder Waldhaus had sprouted. It didn't take much more for it to grow.

Dad died on a Saturday. He was walking home from the local down the road when he collapsed with a massive heart attack, right on the spot where his old pub had stood.

Mum and Dad had retired by then. They'd sold the new pub but kept the Honegger house. My sister's family had restored the top floor and the attic and lived there now. They called me at home, and I rushed back. The family doctor lived right across the street. He organised a stretcher to carry Dad home. By the time I arrived, Dad was laid out on the couch in his office, the bear cave, Mum used to call it.

A nurse asked me to help shift him, to give him a final wash. She told me I could leave, but I didn't. I stayed until they carried him out, watching him fall to the end, like his old pub.

He'd had a smaller heart attack before. We knew he was on borrowed time, but he never changed his lifestyle. It was the way he'd wanted to go.

Janine and the children were there by then, along with the rest of the family. Comfort in numbers works wonders. Of course we were all sad as could be, but somehow it felt like a generous end, a final flash without suffering, and picking the perfect forever moment: he'd come full circle back to his father's pub.

I only shed a tear later, after the shock had worn off, writing his obituary for the pastor to read out.

FOREVER DAY

And just like the time Dad's castle had fallen, I took off, with the family this time. We drove to England and rented a cottage on a farm in East Grinstead for a month. It was one of the hottest summers on record, the tar stuck to your shoes. Hot and dry as a camel's fart, which reminded us where we should have stayed.

There was no phone in the cottage, and the TV had poor reception. We went to town and bought a blow-up plunge pool and a charcoal barbecue. Janine invited her friend's family over, they happened to be holidaying in London at the time. We sweated through a hot Barbie and jumped into the rubber pool. We felt like we were back in the heart of Australia.

We were back on a hundred acres, the children feeding Minties to Dolly, the farmer's tame sheep. Not the one they cloned years later, but it looked exactly the same.

We toured the country, went to the seaside, and took the train into London. We stayed at the Drury Lane Moat House Hotel, the place I always used when visiting for more than a day. Just a minute or two from our High Holborn office, and right across the road from the New London Theatre, where Cats premiered in 1981 and kept the Jellicles meowing and Grizabella belting out *Memory* on a full moon. For an astonishing nine thousand performances.

It had been my night's entertainment on business trips. Now, with the family, we got front-row seats, cats rubbing and bunting all over the kids.

I never even looked at our office up the road. I wondered if Dad had felt like this, feeling the end looming. Fight on or succumb?

FOREVER DAY

I had to hop over to Zollikon for the monthly close. When I came back, Janine sat me down for a talk. She knew the signs. The seed of doubt had grown into a tree. I wasn't happy.

She'd forgiven me my trespasses, but she didn't need another one. I'd had my ride on the wild dragon and left her to cope. She didn't want us to be happy for just one holiday month.

'I'm going back, Flicks.'

'I'm coming, too.'

28

The best laid plans of mice and men

Dad left each of us a house in Switzerland. I rented mine out for a while, then eventually sold it. I only ever went back to Switzerland once, to bury Mum. After her death, apart from my sister, there was nothing worth going back to.

I still think of Switzerland as a picture-perfect, chocolate-box country. But not as my home anymore. Sometimes I dream of it, but not the way you'd think. I dream, for some wild reason, that I'm forced to go back and live there for good.

We made Queensland our new home state. Two of Janine's sisters had settled around Brisbane, so we figured we might as well join them there.

I didn't have a clue what to do next. I had enough cash to buy a house outright and pay the bills for quite some time, but doing nothing was never an option for me. Chickens, newspapers, money laundering and accounting were out. Been there, done that.

In hindsight, I could've kept going for another ten years or more. René Rivkin certainly did. They eventually nabbed him, not for that, but for insider trading, and a pittance at that. By then, the Swiss had changed their banking laws, and the free transfer of cash had changed with them.

Yet even then, and despite legal challenges, the Swiss authorities refused to force the banks to reveal where the missing eleven million dollars from Rivkin's estate went. The Australian authorities decided not to pursue legal action, too costly, too uncertain.

FOREVER DAY

None of the many well-known, high-end Australian Rivkin customers ever got prosecuted. And despite claims to the contrary, money laundering through Swiss banks is still easy, if you've got a local contact.

I don't want to prove it to you, so don't call me.

My brother Luke, his wife Marianne, and their three boys joined us on a family assisted visa I had to sign for in 1991. They'd always dreamed of emigrating to Tuscany, but after comparing house prices, they settled for Australia, back then one of the most affordable places for housing in the developed world.

Whatever happened?

Luke and the family bought a high-set Queenslander in the hills near Fernvale. He was a family man now, but inside, still the carefree spirit from the past.

I remember him taking off to make a career as a painter in France. Rented a small flat, cut off his ear, painted feet with faces, and suffered from malnutrition like Vincent van Gogh. Well, he didn't cut off his ear. I made that up. But he should have. It would've got him into a hospital bed to rest.

He got kicked out of his flat for unpaid rent and somehow still had enough money to ring me for help. I drove my Renault through the night to rescue him, huddled on the steps of his apartment building with the few things they'd let him keep.

Somehow, Luke always landed on his feet. He was a fully trained interior decorator, though I honestly don't know how he made it through four years of apprenticeship, let alone passed his final exams, in a haze of LSD and mescaline.

FOREVER DAY

He landed a dream job with Charles Vögele, owner of the Seedamm Centre on the far side of the lake. The kind of man who wanted his taps gilded and his bedroom walls wallpapered in silk. He was also an art lover, and had a big cultural centre, the *Vögele Kultur Zentrum*. built close to his shopping mall.

Luke told me about the day they put the final touches on a Henry Moore sculpture exhibition. Now Henry was a tweedy sort of English artist, known for hammering out sculptures from seriously big and heavy stone. The one I remember was a reclining monster of a woman no sane man would ever date. I can't recall how much she weighed, probably tons, but they needed a massive crane just to get her into place.

Once she was settled on the floor, Henry stepped up, placed his knee on the stone, and gave it a theatrical nudge, as if adjusting her position.

'That's perfect, now,' he said as if his muse had been waiting for his touch all along.

By now, Luke had been clean for a long time. He'd sold his house in Switzerland and had banked enough money to start over with his family in Australia. For once, the two of us were in the same position, looking for something new to do.

We settled on buying the Wivenhoe Gallery in Fernvale, a small tourist town nestled in the hills near the Wivenhoe Dam. The building had once been the old town hall, complete with a kitchen at the back and a modest stage for the band. In its heyday, it hosted weekend bush dances, the kind with tinnies from eskies, lamingtons in Tupperware containers and a local band playing Slim Dusty covers with a guitar and an out of tune piano.

FOREVER DAY

The woman who sold it to us had converted the old hall into an art gallery. She suffered from MS and never quite managed to finish the job. Luke and I had the means, and the stubborn determination, to complete it for her.

We commissioned a dozen or more artists to display their work. Some pieces we bought outright; others we took on consignment. Not just paintings, we welcomed pottery, silk art, toys, a few sculptures. Anything pretty or unusual made the cut.

We ran ads on Ipswich's QFM, 106.9 FM, and got our business on the map. We cleaned the place up, sanded and polished the hardwood floorboards, made it all look pretty and inviting, then waited for the crowds to show up.

Only a trickle came. Curious onlookers wandered in, wondering why anyone would display paintings in an old hall in a two-horse town. The local real estate guy ambled down from his office, took a look around, and told us we were ahead of our time. He left his card in case we ever felt like selling.

He wasn't the only one. A group of young folks arrived with cameras, location scouts from Warner Bros. Movie World on the Gold Coast. They were looking to rent a picturesque hall just like ours for a planned film. They were happy to put the contents in storage for the duration of the shoot. I gave them a figure that included projected loss of income.

That was the last we heard from them. I might've been a bit optimistic about the income. Old habits die hard.

Fernvale was, and still is, a touristy little place, known for its Sunday market in the school grounds and a bakery that sells the famous Fernvale pie.

FOREVER DAY

We were tucked a bit back from the main road, but people would grab a pie and wander down into our hall, munching as they went, leaving gravy and tomato sauce fingerprints across our displays. Some didn't even pretend to browse; they just came in to use the toilets.

Weekends got a lot busier. Luke and I would rise at first light and head to Wivenhoe Dam for a spot of fishing before opening the shop for weekend trade. It felt like the old days at Lake Zurich, just on the other side of the world. When Luke moved up to the Sunshine Coast, he switched from freshwater to salt. I never made the transition.

We bought a yearly permit to fish the lake. It came with a pamphlet listing the stocked species and a stern warning: a $60,000 fine for catching the endangered Australian lungfish. Guess what Luke hooked on our first outing? A lungfish. What are the odds! It was a great game fish, shot up like a Blue Marlin. Luke reeled it in and let it go. After that, it was mostly fork-tailed blue catfish.

I wanted to taste one, so I banged its head on a rock a couple of times. When we were done, I took it back to the gallery and dropped it in the kitchen sink. Halfway through the morning, I heard it flapping. Talk about a thick skull. Mum would've soaked it in milk water for a couple of days first, but I just wanted to taste it as it was: rubbery, with a muddy tang. Janine, who grew up with flake, flathead and leatherjacket, banned it from the kitchen thereafter.

During the slack times on week days, I retreated to the backroom and resumed my old hobby, building wooden model boats. I also fired up the PC, determined to launch my writing career properly this time. Just before leaving Switzerland, I'd stitched up a deal for three more YA books with Aare Verlag Solothurn. I'd already written two for them, one, *Survivors*, did well enough to get picked up by MacMillan in London and a handful of foreign publishers. My plan was modest: keep writing, make some petty cash, and let the boats float.

I finished the first of the three contracted books and sent the manuscript off on a floppy disk. It floated off like a message in a bottle. No word back. I was busy with the gallery and didn't worry too much. A year passed. I tried to contact them. Phones dead. No trace of Aare Verlag. I never saw a red cent in royalties or even a Christmas card. I had simply ceased to exist.

There's a new Aare Verlag now, operating out of another Swiss town. They're not successors, just recyclers of the name. Water under the Aare River.

One door closes, another opens, and sometimes, the Gods smile and open the very door that leads you down a road you didn't know existed.

Most of our clients were women. From the counter by the door, I could see their husbands parked outside in the car, smoking their boredom away. I gave it some thought. What would get a man into the shop? Shiny things. Brass. Metal. Wood. Tools.

I put it to the test straight away. I cleared two shelves right by the entry. On the top shelf, I placed my finished wooden model boats, the *Endeavour* and the *Mississippi Queen*, as bait. Below, I filled every inch with vintage tools: blow torches, plumb bobs, boxwood and brass rules, levels, hand planes, drills, saws, all scavenged from the ten or so antique shops that operated in and around Ipswich back then.

FOREVER DAY

It made a very impressive display. And it worked a treat. I didn't even have to advertise it. The female customers did it all for me. They got hubby into the shop, free to browse on their side, in their own time, without the car horn summoning them back like errant schoolchildren.

I was Captain Cook once more, turning my boat on a hunch and discovering a new continent: vintage hand tools. They winked at me like Janine on The Love Boat, many years before.

I went full bore, for the next thirty years, buying and selling things I liked, loving every minute of it. I never thought a single day of it was work.

Dad would have approved.

My brother Luke followed suit. He too, stumbled over the threshold of a new door: opals, precious and semi-precious gems. I think he bought a bag of low-grade stones from a shop on the way to the Sunshine Coast, during a beach outing. For Luke, that trip opened a double-door: opals and the Sunshine Coast. He moved his family there two years later.

By then, he'd registered a claim in Lightning Ridge, digging with a retired accountant from Sydney he'd met in town. Like everyone else, they were hoping to strike the big one: a black opal. Few ever did.

Most of the opals Luke brought home, he'd bought from other miners. He kept the good ones and practiced cutting and polishing on the dime-a-dozen stuff. He reckoned mastering the art of a good cut was worth more than digging dirt. He must have been pretty good at it because a year or so after, he went to a big gemstone trade show in Germany and sold most of his inventory.

FOREVER DAY

He had a backroom in his house rigged with cutting, polishing, and cabbing wheels, spraying water and sand all over the walls. A large rotating contraption tumbled pebbles and semi-precious stones until they came out shiny, like the back of a cockroach. He once threw in one of my old spanners and made it look brand new. He was pleased with the result. I didn't see the point. Why make an old tool look like new?

After we sold the gallery and he'd moved away, we drifted apart, by distance and interests. We met for Christmas and family events, always with the children in tow; once went camping and walking in the lush rainforest in Lamington National Park. The kids were bitten by so many leeches they looked like they'd been peppered with buckshot from a shotgun. We marveled at blue crayfish in the creeks, swam in a waterhole with eels that were frighteningly big. They were used to human interaction, loved egg and lettuce sandwiches and left us in peace.

Luke and Marianne seemed happy enough with their lives down under. There was just one warning sign, and we all missed it.

Luke dropped in unannounced and asked if Marianne had called in by any chance. He reckoned she'd gone back to their old house, which sounded odd. When I asked why, he shrugged. 'She's done that before,' he said. And stupid knucklehead me let it go.

A few months later, early morning, he rang.

'Marianne is gone,' he said.

'Gone where? Back to the house?'

'She's dead,' he said. 'Killed herself on the back veranda with a rope.'

I'll never forget that fist of ice that grips you from head to toe. You know it's true, but you don't want to.

'Can you come and get the boys? The police wants me to stay put.'

I rushed up to the Coast as fast as I could. Two and a half hours. Plenty of time to rack your brain and dig through your thoughts. Sweet, placid Marianne, who made beautiful toys and sold them through a gift shop. At the end of a rope?

It beggared belief. But over every other thought was the one that wouldn't leave me: Why had I missed it? Why had we all?

Luke was in a daze as he showed me the spot. He'd cut her off when he found her in early hours. Luckily the boys were fast asleep. He called the police and they informed the coroner. There is a protocol to follow and thank God they were really quick and professional about it. Marianne had climbed on a chair, bound her hands and fell, leaving a bible open with a passage that didn't hold a clue, just like she'd opened up the book of her own life, written in a language we didn't understand.

I took the boys home, stopped on the way for breakfast, and told them, again and again, what happened to your mum is not your fault. They stayed with us for a while, played with our children, seemed to take it in okay.

It took a long time for the coroner to release Marianne's body. After the funeral, Luke packed up the house and left for Switzerland.

FOREVER DAY

Two of his boys came back later, young men on holiday, to fit out a van in our backyard and tour Australia. They were naturalised Australians and had always dreamed of returning for good. But all their love of sand and surf couldn't erase the fact that their mother had come here to die.

My brother and I lost contact for twenty years or more. He came back for a visit once after that. 'To make peace with Marianne,' he said. I think he found it, up the hill by the creek with the turtles, where they'd started out. He went there looking for gems in the water.

He told me they'd taken Marianne's ashes home for a funeral at her parents' place. Her father had said, "You've taken her to Australia to die."

Luke returned to the opal fields. His claim had long expired, but he teamed up with another miner once more. When he was done, he disappeared. Said he was looking after a small farm back in Switzerland, sleeping in a caravan left behind by a circus clown.

It would be another fifteen years before my sister found him again, settled contently in an apartment in the town where he'd married Marianne.

I know there was undiagnosed trouble that ran in her family. Still, unspoken between us lingered our guilt. I should have read the signs. But he, of all people, should have known.

29

The rusty bits are in the back

There's something about old hand tools that stirs the dust of memory, like unearthed artefacts or secret stones left in the folds of time for us to discover. You pick up an old tool and feel the hands that held it before.

I felt it first, early on, in a cooper's wooden downright shave, its handles worn with deep thumb and finger indents where the worker had gripped it for years. It offered a glint into the looking glass, back to my parents' first pub, with the smithy on one side and Mr Lehmann's workshop on the other.

Mr Lehmann was a cooper and a wheelwright, though few people needed wooden barrels or wagon wheels anymore. He still made new barrels now and then, or repaired broken staves and hoops. Occasionally, he'd fix a wheel for a horse buggy or a vintage car with wooden spokes. The rest of the time he mended wagons and trays. He was a miracle woodworker. He never seemed to measure anything, yet everything fit. He'd cut and plane the staves of a barrel and fit them watertight, just by holding them up and squinting.

He had no children of his own, we were all his children. He let us stay in his workshop all day, handing us a piece of wood and a plane, letting us chatter it across the surface until the cutting edge was as blunt as a twenty-cent coin. Then he'd sharpen it on a whetstone, slow and deliberate, like Luke eating his lunch.

Everything Mr Lehmann built took its time to last. Only Mr Lehmann didn't last that long. He closed his workshop years before we moved down to the lake. He went to work for a joinery that made kitchens.

I know it wasn't his plane I picked up. But it could have been.

We sold the Wivenhoe gallery building to an antique dealer and Luke and his family moved on. I was left with a garage full of paintings, pottery, knickknacks, most of which I donated to our children's school for their annual fundraiser.

That left me with eight large, hand-crafted silky oak display cabinets with glass shelves, and the most precious thing I'd acquired in three years of selling: a tested, proven fact. Vintage hand tools sell like hotcakes. No doubt about it.

To turn that into a business, I had to take a leaf out of Al Neuharth's playbook: Think big. Buy bigger.

If you've got a commodity in high demand, you need a matching supply to keep the wheels turning. I wasn't the first Australian dealer of antique tools, but I was the first to make it a full-time, standalone business. Selling was easy. Finding the merchandise? Much harder than I'd imagined.

I'm constantly amused when I tell people what I do for a living. They say, "You must've gone to a lot of flea markets and garage sales." True, but mostly for fun. I rarely picked up anything that would pay the bills. One-hundred-year-old tools are rare by design. You don't stumble across them in a garage sale in a brand-new estate.

Yet I met collectors who'd built substantial holdings from flea markets, swap meets, and garage sales. It takes a lot of travel and a lifetime of sifting through boxes of crap. One man's collection isn't a business. But thirty collectors' worth of effort might be.

FOREVER DAY

Three things became clear:

One: if I wanted to make a decent living from vintage tools, I had to scale up the buying.

Two: nobody was going to teach me how. I'd have to figure it out myself.

Three: there weren't enough antique tools in all of Australia to make it work.

It became glaringly obvious during my first two years of trading: I couldn't sit in a shop and wait for customers to clear out the shelves. I had to be on the road, filling them.

After Luke and I sold the hall and parted ways, I moved my eight silky oak display cases into Neil Hagan's antique shop at the foot of the Toowoomba Range. Neil was old-school, a gentleman tradesman with a fourth-generation cabinetmaking and French polishing pedigree. His son, David, took over the furniture business while Neil set up the antique shop as his retirement project.

He'd done well in the crazy '80s, when excess ruled and Australia printed money to burn. By the time I came along in the early '90s, the country was still reeling from recession. Unemployment had hit 11%. Neil was happy to try something new and sell my tools on commission.

It cut my shop time down to once a week. I'd restock the shelves, we'd drink coffee and yarn, and he'd tell me how he and his father had polished everything from grand pianos in the Festival Centre to sideboards in Brisbane Town Hall. Neil inspired me to start working with wood myself. I never reached his level of perfection, but I gave it a go. My first project was to remodel an old sideboard into a display cabinet for the two model ships I'd

FOREVER DAY

salvaged from the Fernvale display. Neil sold the whole lot, for a month's wages, to a Sydney Harbour restaurateur, who installed it in his maritime-themed dining room.

Once a month on my Mondays, while I cleaned my display, the pre-loved jewellery salesman would call. I remember him vividly. He dressed like Al Capone. When he opened his case to take out trays of precious rings, necklaces and brooches, he first had to remove a loaded gun sitting on top of the lot. Al Capone, the jewellery salesman, had a license to carry.

Years later, I'd be hauling trays of vintage tools for my mate Mike Urness in the USA, same setup, loaded gun on top. No license to match.

I loved my Mondays with Neil.

I loved my Tuesdays at home and my Wednesdays on the road. I'd mapped out a round-trip that looped through dozens of antique shops from Northern New South Wales to Bundaberg. Back then, any fair-sized town had several. These days, you're lucky to find one within reach.

I got to know the owners. They kept the good stuff for me, under the counter. Whenever I walked into a new establishment and asked if they had any tools for sale, the answer was always the same:

"The rusty bits are in the back."

By about this time I sold the house Dad had left me in Switzerland and built a new brick family home on one and a quarter acres, twenty bathrooms to outdo Al's. Just kidding. Five bedrooms and a whopping great big heated pool. Now you might think that's extravagant in sun-drenched Queensland, but winters can get cold. Kind of. All it did was raise the temps and push the twelve-metre pool into spa territory. Our youngest, Mike, would check the water and declare anything under forty degrees Celsius unfit for a swim.

Now that we had finally landed on our home turf, we got seriously domestic. Two dogs, three cats, ten guinea pigs and a flock of chooks, a dam with a bridge over the water, full of fish and yabbies, a ride-on mower and a large shed with an air-conditioned office for dad's tools. Domestic bliss. Not as fancy as it might sound, but a perfect picture of the Australian dream.

We loved our chooks, and they loved us back, because we were beautiful people. I can prove it. No chicken shit.

"Chickens Prefer Beautiful Humans." That's the title of a Swedish study by Stockholm University's Zoology Department and the Group for Interdisciplinary Cultural Research, published in Human Nature in 2002. The researchers trained chickens to peck at images of human faces in exchange for food. First, they used average-looking faces. Then they gave the birds a choice. The chickens consistently pecked the beautiful ones.

There you have it. Forget the mirror. If you want to know your place in the beauty pecking order, ask a chicken.

One of our dogs was a Doberman named Max, the smartest animal we ever had. I've met dumber humans. When we let the chickens out for a lawn peck, Max made sure they stayed well clear of the house. We only had to shush them away a couple of times before Max took it on as his personal mission.

Our children loved playing with their guinea pigs. I built an apartment block to house them all, out of an old wardrobe. One of the litter was deformed, with short front legs and probably deaf and blind. The kids named him Puzzle, put him in their remote-controlled toy car, and whizzed him around the yard.

One day, Puzzle disappeared probably fell out of the cage. Max found him and brought him back, licked wet but perfectly fine. This was Max, who used to jump on rats and kill them with one shake of his head. He knew Puzzle was family. And family had to be protected.

To find the tools I needed in Australia, I had to pay top dollar. Most dealers offered me their best stock, and I paid whatever they asked. I'm not talking hundreds. I mean thousands. I once bought a single tool chest, packed to the brim, from an antique dealer in Toowoomba for fifteen grand. It filled just one of Neil's display cabinets.

My reasoning was simple: I couldn't be the only fool willing to pay what it takes. I spent a fortune doing it. Made little in return. But I got to handle tools few collectors had ever touched. I learned a lot. Made contacts that proved invaluable, none more so than Paul Withers and Mike Urness.

My first four years of tax returns looked like Alex the Hungarian's. I spent money like Zoltan.

Let me pause here and offer some advice you probably don't want to hear: Tool dealing in Australia isn't a stellar business. It just pays the bills. That said, I'm eternally grateful I stumbled into it. Not once did I think of it as work. It suited me, and what I wanted out of life. No boring routine. No nine-to-five. No boss breathing down my neck. No well-trodden path. No safety net. Just the kind of challenge that keeps me going.

My first buying trip to England was in the mid-'90s. I rented a wagon, bought three large wooden tool chests, and zigzagged from a shop in Bournemouth across England to David Stanley's auction, Tony Murland's and Roy Arnold's shop in Needham Market, and all the way up to Scotland's Inchmartine Tool Bazaar, stopping at every antique shop and fair between them. Two weeks later, I had three trunks full of quality tools. I drove them to my Australian import company's Heathrow freight forwarder and had them flown home. By the time I landed, they were already at Australian customs awaiting fumigation.

Earlier on, I bumped into Reg Eaton and his wife at a tool sale in Sydney. I only learned more about him after the fact, and was amazed to discover how much we had in common. He'd sold his woodworking business and gone looking for something else to do. When I later visited him at his home in King's Lynn, he told me he'd either bought, or meant to buy, a pub. I'm still not sure which. In any case, he'd been collecting things all his life and eventually decided to make tools his full-time trade.

It's no stretch to call him the grandfather of English tool dealers. He had at least a dozen years' head start on me, and he must have come to the same conclusion I did: to buy and sell, you've got to be on the road.

Reg sold a lot of tools down under, either by shipping directly and sidestepping duties, or through antique centres that took his stock on consignment. I believe he had a major falling-out with at least one of them, which may have prompted his trip to the Sydney tool sale, where he flogged off a substantial chunk of his Australian inventory.

When I heard about it after the sale, I tried to contact him with an offer to buy the lot. But he was travelling constantly and never got the message. Funny enough, Neil later told me Reg had actually visited the shop to check out my tools at the very time I tried to get hold of him.

In the end, Reg sold his entire Australian stock through general auction houses in the major cities. I went to the Brisbane one and bought the lot, for surprisingly little money.

When I finally caught up with Reg in England, he tried to gloss over it, but I got the sense he was done dealing down under for good. I didn't want to show off and tell him, but I was sure I was going to fill the void.

Reg didn't have much stock left at his place. In fact, his large workshop was all but empty, except for a pile of Gunther-type surveyors' chains, boxed and ready to ship to the USA. Apparently, there was big money in them at the time. I never asked, but I assumed most of his income came from American buyers. I know he sold through David Stanley in England as well. At one sale, Reg's son John put up a very rare early English plough plane he'd picked up for a fiver. It sold for several thousand pounds. We all heard him singing out with joy from the back row, then storming out of the auction house to put a deposit on a car, or so my neighbour said.

Reg did sell me some of the stock he'd meant to take to a Midwest Tool Club sale in the USA. I can't remember exactly what I bought, but I do recall one item clearly: a mint, empty box for a Stanley 1.

Reg, of course, was world-renowned for his expertise on Ultimatum braces. His living room walls were covered with them. He'd authored the definitive book on the subject: *The Ultimate Brace: A Unique Product of Victorian Sheffield (1998)*.

FOREVER DAY

I was impressed by how Reg presented his tools. Clean, waxed, some polished, but still retaining their age. I asked him what his secret was. He showed me his buffing wheel. I went home and bought one, too.

Not all collectors agreed with Reg's shine. But I didn't care. Some American collectors used to call me "the Aussie Reg Eaton" later on. I wore the badge with pride. I could make the rusty bits look better, and they would sell.

30

Tools from the Sky

We were preparing for our first tool auction, held in the old hall at the Rosewood showground. It featured some of the best tools I'd sourced over the past year. We hired a local auctioneer. Janine, Lucy with a friend and our eldest daughter, Corinne, ran the office. My brother-in-law and a few helpers manned the pick-up desk. It all went swimmingly. The hall was packed, the auction a great success.

I'd invited a few fellow dealers to sell their gear on the side, just like the car park sale at David Stanley's auction in England, but done the Australian way: inside the hall, alongside the main event, like a sideshow at Ringling Brothers.

Some of the dealers slept over in the hall, curled up between the tables with the lots all laid out. After everything was ready for the show, we headed to the local for a meal and a few drinks. That's where I met Les, an old codger with a toothless grin, who told me the story about fish falling from the sky. I don't know why he picked me. Maybe because I was born in a pub, and had that look etched into my face. The look of someone who'd listen.

Les recalled the day he walked home from school along the Minden–Rosewood Road, just after a big afternoon thunderstorm. There, in the roadside ditches in great puddles of water across the fields, he spotted them, many hundreds of tiny fish, maybe an inch long. Flickering in the water like silver confetti. He reckoned they'd fallen with the rain. Straight from the sky.

It was one of those stories you don't quite get until you remember it later. Fish from the sky? I could do one better: a 20mm cannon cartridge shell, falling out of a clear blue sky and landing in the Hotel Lion's kitchen vegetable patch. I'm sure Les' story was true, but so is mine.

As a boy, I never thought to ask: where the hell had it come from? I didn't see a thing until it hit the ground.

Much later, remembering it as an adult, I could piece it together. The shell case had most likely been ejected from one of the four 20mm cannons in the nose of a de Havilland Venom fighter jet. Back then, the Swiss Air Force used to fire live rounds at floating practice targets in the nearby lake. They'd cordon off one end for target practice, peppering the floats with 20mm shells, while families swam and paddled at the other. Talk about integrating your armed forces into civilian life.

On the other side of the world and a century earlier, chunks of meat fell from the blue sky over Kentucky. No warning, no storm, just flesh, raining down. Some folks fried it. No, it didn't taste like chicken. More like venison, or some other wild game. Scientists ran tests. They confirmed it was meat, but the mystery lingered until years later, when an ornithologist offered a theory: the meat was the regurgitated stomach contents of vultures, soaring so high they couldn't be seen from the ground. When vultures get spooked, they vomit to lighten their load and escape faster. And apparently, if one blows lunch, the rest follow. Thus: The Kentucky meat shower.

Where was I? Ah yes, the mythical meaning some events take on over time. Like our first tool shower. I still hear from people who travelled hundreds, even thousands of miles, and recall details from that day I can't. Compared to David Stanley or Bud Brown, our sale was small fry. It wasn't the first of its kind down under, but it was, without doubt, the finest mix of quality tools ever offered at auction with a fully illustrated catalogue in Australia to that point. There would be plenty more to come.

Things accelerated at break-neck speed. The internet cracked open commercially, and it happened right in my hometown. The tectonic shift of our generation, right there, between the pool, the Barbie, and the static hiss turned metallic wail of a 50k modem.

Janine and Coleen, bored stiff by the male tech talk, got gloriously drunk and cannonballed into the pool fully clothed. Five kids followed suit into aquatic anarchy. I was the designated driver, three precious in the back, stone sober and wide-eyed. Good thing too, because at the Kenny's party in Karana Downs, I found myself deep in conversation with Mal Bryce, Scott Balson, and a local councillor, the founding fathers of GIL. That chat re-wired my business model on the spot.

After fleeing the Western Australian Burke corruption scandal in which he was not involved, Mal Bryce, ex-Deputy Premier turned civic Prometheus, landed in Ipswich, Queensland, armed with a vision: transform the town's new library from punch card to portal. The plan? A wide-area network where ratepayers could pay bills, check library books, and commune with the future.

Enter Scott Balson, techno-seer with a prototype and a breakfast invite. In early 1994, he demoed his interactive system, part Mosaic, part municipal oracle, to Bryce and the Ipswich brass. The council blinked, nodded, and handed him and Bryce the reins. Thus was born Global Info-Links or GIL, Australia's first internet service, stitched together from Balson's West Australian blueprint and Bryce's bureaucratic redemption arc.

By February 1995, Barry Jones unveiled a pyramid to commemorate the ground breaking task, wooden base, acrylic head, names etched like civic runes. Pauline Hanson, then a councillor, denounced the $17 million library as a waste of roads and rubbish. Ironically, she became Australia's first cyber-politician thanks to the very system she scorned.

GIL was the shining light of internet invention but ten years later the politicians moved in and wrecked it all. Mayor Underwood lost his seat. Paul Pisasale rose, ousted Bryce, and claimed the pyramid as his own. By 1997, the monument was landfill. By 1999, Pisasale was linked to an online casino and was eventually jailed many years later, on some other dishonesty charges. He's still referred to as the guy who put Ipswich on the map, still liked by many. Bloody fool had it all and blew it. Too cocky for his own good.

I was one of the first commercial users to drag my business into cyberspace. Bought Microsoft FrontPage, designed the site myself, back when "design" meant tables, blinking text, and praying the GIFs loaded. It worked. Most of the time.

Thirty years later, I shut it down. By then it was a digital labyrinth: twenty thousand pictures, a spiderweb of pages, and a backend held together by extinct code and sheer willpower. The program had long ceased to exist. I hadn't. But it was bloody hard work in the end.

The move online was a quantum leap, and it came just in time. Neil's shop went under. The bank called in his business loan the moment he turned seventy. Too old to run a business, they said. He'd put up his house and the shop as security. Couldn't raise the funds, so they took the lot. House gone. Business gone. Another life wrecked in the name of "good business." One more reason I'd vowed, long ago, never to depend on the man again.

FOREVER DAY

Neil rang me just days before the receivers moved in. His son managed to rescue the stock, good stock, too, and I kept mine. In Neil's shop, it would've taken a year to shift. Online, it was gone in a month.

Enter Mike Urness from St. Louis, Missouri. A few years my junior, but we could've been twins in temperament and taste. He'd ridden the dragon on Mississippi barges in his youth, plea-bargained away his licence after a string of DUIs, then gave up drinking but never gave up driving. My kind of Ned Kelly civil disobedience. They arrested him once, years later, out of state, thought they'd caught a fugitive. Bureaucratic bungle. Gave him a fright, I'm sure, but he walked.

Mike loved his Harley Davidson and Indian bikes, his sushi, and what he called 'the cute little redhead from Bud Brown's auction', Miss Kitty, whom he eventually married. He should've been a chef, the way he talked about food. Whenever I landed Stateside, he'd have the eateries lined up like a tasting menu. I never tried his sushi, but his banana bread was legendary.

We shared a love of writing too. He edited his college newsletter, wrote about rock music, then drifted into country.

I think we met through the *Electronic Neanderthal Woodworker*, that primordial website listing U.S. tool dealers and vintage hand tool lore. There weren't many of us back then. Mike didn't run a site with pictures, just Spartan lists. That's how we connected, and I'm eternally grateful we did.

For the next twenty-five years, Mike was more than a supplier, he was my point man and my friend in the States. I lost count of the parcels sent to his mum's address. He'd pack them in K-Mart tubs or cardboard boxes, wrapped in miles of duct tape like Egyptian mummies. My forwarder would scoop them up and airfreight them to Brisbane.

Janine was collecting My Little Ponies back then. She'd buy the rare ones in the U.S. and have them shipped to Mike, nestled between Stanley planes and corner drills. Australia Quarantine rang me once, puzzled: "What's with the little horses?"

Eventually Mike started his own auctions and still trades as Great Planes Trading Co. He came to one of my Rosewood auctions and fell in love with Four'n Twenty Pies. I packed a couple when we met at Bud Brown's auction near Hershey's Chocolate Wonderland. Had them warmed in the hotel kitchen, but after the long haul they weren't quite as crisp as they came out of the cornershop warmer down under. Still, they did the job. Pastry diplomacy sealed the bond.

That 1996 auction was memorable for two reasons.

First: the Tidy plough plane. Ebony and brass, polished to a Reg Eaton gleam, some said too polished, but I didn't care. It fetched $27,500, a new record. We all clapped, then looked at each other like we'd just witnessed a unicorn sale. Somebody thought it was worth that much, and that was that.

Second: John Walter launched the second edition of the Stanley Bible. *Antique & Collectible Stanley Tools: Guide to Identity & Value.* Everyone bought a copy. The side-dealers bolted back to the sales room to mark up their prices. What made it truly momentous wasn't the launch, but the fact that it would remain the last update for the next thirty years. Dozens of promises, no new edition. If we'd known, we'd have bought the lot. They were twenty bucks a copy, signed if you asked. Today they fetch ten times that, if you can find one.

FOREVER DAY

American auctions were a hoot. I never quite knew what the hammer price was, the auctioneer was always an increment ahead, singing and yodelling all at once. Somehow, I always ended up paying less than I thought.

What struck me most was the trust. Once the hammer fell, helpers would bring your lot and place it right at your feet, trusting you'd pay on the way out.

When I started selling tools at various venues, I experienced that gentleman's trust among American tool guys firsthand. I'd arrive with four large bags packed with my best. I'd put the first lot on the sales table, bend down for the next, and when I stood up again, I nearly fainted. Most of my tools were gone.

Mike told me not to worry. 'They'll come and fix you up later.' Believe me, I did worry. I might as well not have rented a table. They virtually took the tools straight out of my bag and stashed them under their own sales tables so nobody else could get their hands on them.

They were good tools, no doubt, but priced very low. I'd left my Australian sales stickers on them, priced in Aussie dollars. They paid in US dollars, which was nearly double. I went home with so much cash I had to declare it to customs. They had a hard time believing I made it from old tools.

I felt Zoltan's ghost turn in its grave.

Janine came with me to one of the Midwest Tool Club sales in Omaha, Nebraska, held in a sprawling hotel that smelled faintly of waffles and stale coffee.

Before that, we'd done the tourist circuit in LA: Disneyland, Universal Studios, the celebrity home tours. We even counted most of the stars in the pavement along the Hollywood Walk of Fame, Janine's trip down memory lane and the hours after school, watching black and white movies on TV until Mum came home.

Once settled in Omaha, we spread the tools across the humongously big bed Americans love, wide enough to host a summit, and opened the hotel door. That's how dealing was done. No booth, no banner, just a bed full of tools and an open door policy.

I ventured out to buy. Janine stayed behind, perched on the bed, flicking through a hundred channels of American television and selling tools on the side.

Good times. And they kept coming.

There were many more trips to the USA and England over the next two decades. Slowly, the scene shifted. Tool dealing became a serious business for many, some backed by cashed-up collectors with deep pockets and sharper elbows.

I was happy to stay the course and do my own thing. I'd found my forever days in life and work. Why rock the boat when the sailing was clear?

It paid the bills right through to retirement. But let me just say: the mythical lure and wonder of those first three or four years could never be repeated. Tools from the sky.

31

Home Run

The Australian tool establishment didn't exactly welcome me with open arms.

There were two major tool clubs, one in Melbourne, the other in Sydney. I was a newcomer in every sense of the word. A new Australian, as the term goes. And a new breed of tool guy: not a collector, not a tradesman, just the bloke who bought their tools and made them more expensive for everyone else. Fair enough. As I say to anyone who doesn't like my tools, my writing, or just my face:

Make your own.

Of course, there were exceptions, too many to name, but chief among them were Henry Black in Sydney, Paul Withers in Adelaide, and Jim Black, whom I met at the Melbourne sale. Jim was a noted collector who also traded on the side, crisscrossing Australia in search of bargains. At the time, he had the sharpest eye in the business.

Paul Withers was the deliberate type. Some people call that slow. He never fooled me. He had a keen eye, picked up fantastic bargains, and passed them on to me. He never reached the overseas volumes, but he turned out to be a true friend, one who gave me exceptionally good tools and even better leads. We visited each other over the years and attended tool sales all over the country.

Eventually, I began travelling to the Sydney and Melbourne tool sales too. They couldn't bloody well ignore me any longer.

FOREVER DAY

I had the goods.

Janine often joined me for the two-day drive to Melbourne. We'd set up on Saturday, sell on Sunday, then I'd drive her to the airport for her flight home. I ended up driving the car back solo, 1,800 kilometres of road and financial regret. I got so many speeding fines they threatened to take my license.

Janine had to be back for Monday. She'd taken on a one-and-a-half-day job at St Mary's in Ipswich, running the school uniform shop for both the primary school and the college. She stuck it out for twenty-three years.

After she left, it all collapsed. The school outsourced the uniforms to a retail chain. The soul went with her.

We tried to do the math but couldn't be sure. I reckon over the years we took thirty trips to Melbourne and half of that to Sydney for tool sales and many more for family beach holidays in our old stomping ground in Rosebud on Port Phillip Bay. I don't think there is an eatery, a petrol station or a rest room on the Newell Highway we don't know.

When Janine couldn't make it, I'd take my brother-in-law, John. We did most of the Sydney sales together. I won't bore you with them all, but one stands out, unique in every sense.

It wasn't a tool club sale. It was the 1998 *Working With Wood Show*, one of the first events ever held in the brand-new Dome at Sydney Showground, right next to the Olympic stadium, still a year from completion.

I'd reserved a large booth with trestles at enormous cost, without enough tools to fill it. John drove my tool wagon down, loaded to the roof, tires pumped to bursting and still swaying like an overloaded boat. Meanwhile, I jetted off to the Old Devonport Post Office in New Zealand for the Jackson's "Muzeum" auction, containing an amazing 30,000 lots.

The sale was well advertised. I shared the hotel with buyers from all over the world.

There were some decent tools in the lot, but the Kiwi bidders were on fire. I had to pass. So instead of returning to Sydney with bags of bounty, I limped home with hardly anything to show.

But I wasn't done yet.

I'd lined up the purchase of an entire collection in Sydney earlier. With all my cash intact from the New Zealand fail, I drove to the collector's house and bought the lot for cash. It was more than I'd anticipated. We filled the wagon, called two taxis for the surplus, and drove in convoy to the Olympic centre.

We piled the haul onto the tables, twice. It was a two-day event, and we drove home empty.

I bettered my record later at an estate sale.

Flew down to Melbourne, drove back in a rental. It kept beeping at me every two hours until I finally worked out it was a warning to take a break. So I did, and called in on a customer on the way home.

I showed him the best of the lot I had in the car. Among them: three very rare Norris planes, one still in its original box. Funny thing, I'd seen them before. Twelve years earlier, at David Stanley's place in England. He was packing them up, said they were headed to an Australian customer.

FOREVER DAY

I recognised them straight away. The former owner had stamped them: Alvin Sellens, American collector and author of several early tool books. Strange how that plane came back to me, just as I was starting to write tool books myself.

My customer was determined to buy the extra-long Norris jointer plane then and there. I hadn't even thought about pricing.

When I stalled, he asked, 'What would it take?'

'One of my daughters just started uni and needs a new car,' I said, still stalling.

'How much is a new car?'

'Twenty-two thousand,' I said, without thinking.

That's what he paid.

Dumb luck, and a customer who, just then, could well afford it. I believe the tool gods were with me that day.

That one plane was my personal best. Bread-and-butter tools usually averaged around $120 a lot, if the mix was good and I hadn't made too many mistakes.

You only learn from your mistakes in this business. And it takes time. A lot of time.

Time is the least understood dimension.

When you're unhappy, it drags. When you're content, it carries you, season to season.

A warm summer evening on the veranda, your home at your back, your veggie patch at your feet. Autumn fog in the fields, your children flying a kite, your dogs chasing the string.

FOREVER DAY

Winter at the fire pit, roasting chestnuts to remember snow-covered years. It didn't work.

From chicken dance to chicken dance at school, from end-of-year awards to graduation.

Time flies when you stop counting hours and days, it just flows into years of content, but every now and then, it just stops.

When Tara died.

Never married. Mother of four sons. Our Black cousins. Fathers unknown, well, that's what she wrote on the birth certificates, for reasons of her own. She was candid about it. Said she wanted one of each shade, Indigenous all.

Children know no colour unless you paint it for them. We didn't. Tara and her boys fitted in just fine, splashing in the pool, hopping along to all our many dos. When we ran out of family occasions or friends over, Janine called me a stick-in-the-mud and brought a new party home. One great big happy family of equal Australians, right?

Multiculturalism always looks different from the receiving end.

Tara lived it from the bottom up. A lifetime on Centrelink, public housing, and half her years spent socialising at Brothers Leagues Club.

She was easy to talk to. A lovely woman. Not a bad bone in her body. But there must have been demons. Something that drove her to the edge. In the end, she drank herself into hospital, diagnosed with end-stage liver disease.

She died soon after. Just forty-six years young.

FOREVER DAY

St Mary's in Ipswich was packed, like a celebrity's state funeral. Half of Brothers League Club turned out to see her off. She was well liked, loved, and will be sorely missed. But clearly, for her, it wasn't enough.

You pause. You reflect. You move on. There are worse fates than death, a father told me once, when I was cleaning out the USA TODAY office in Guam. He'd shot his son with a bow and arrow. A hunting accident. Killed him dead.

Think too much, and you drift. Return to your happy place. No matter how you deny it, the centre of your universe is always made by you.

Find love and purpose, and all your planets align and orbit in perfect harmony.

Forever Day

Family, woodworking, tools, and writing.

I still do what I love best.

****

FOREVER DAY

FOREVER DAY

Any World (That I'm Welcome To)

If I had my way
I would move to another lifetime
I'd quit my job
Ride the train through the misty nighttime
I'll be ready when my feet touch ground
Wherever I come down
And if the folks will have me
Then they'll have me

Any world that I'm welcome to
Is better than the one I come from

Steely Dan 1975

FOREVER DAY

Epilogue: Fact or Fiction?

Apart from two or three characters, everyone in this story is a real person, and most of the events happened as described and can be verified. The River Woman never existed, but the trip to Lyon was code for a different kind of journey. Yes, I did buy and build up a chicken franchise in Hastings, and I did employ ex-Telecom staff on workers' comp.

The Hungarians are real, apart from Zoltan, who stands in for every other Austral-Hungarian in the network. Yes, I did deposit cash for my friends and invested in futures, and I made enough money out of it to buy a property down under for cash.

The Italian money connection is invented, but the meeting about chicken supplies and seasoning did take place, and the old man did look and act like a mobster. My time with USA TODAY is entirely real and required no embellishment.

As in every autobiography, events may be time-shifted, rearranged, highlighted, or toned down to fit the narrative. My family and I moved house twenty-three times across two continents. In reality, we returned to live in Switzerland twice, not once, and our first two children were born there, not in Australia.

Yes, my first published book was written in the broken-down Morris near Kalgoorlie, and back in Switzerland I found a publisher for that story in record time. I kept writing more books and articles than mentioned here. I never made much money out of it, but I enjoyed every minute.

FOREVER DAY

Thank you for reading all the way to the end.

PS: if you like to keep in touch, join me on Facebook and find out if there are more vintage tools or books coming your way.

https://www.facebook.com/hans.brunner.796

www.ingramcontent.com/pod-product-compliance
Lightning Source LLC
Chambersburg PA
CBHW052015070526
44584CB00016B/1764